SECOND EDITION

THE ULTIMATE MARKETING PLAN

Find your most promotable competitive edge, turn it into a powerful marketing message, and deliver it to the right prospects

DANIEL KENNEDY

Adams Media Corporation
Holbrook, Massachusetts

To Gary Halbert, who is largely responsible for me being in the direct marketing field, an inspiring innovator and a good friend.

Published by
Adams Media Corporation
260 Center Street, Holbrook, MA 02343
www.adamsmedia.com

ISBN: 1-58062-253-4

Printed in Canada

J I H G F E D C B

Library of Congress Cataloging-in-Publication data available
upon request from the publisher.

This publication is designed to provide accurate and authoritative information with regard to the subject matter covered. It is sold with the understanding that the publisher is not engaged in rendering legal, accounting, or other professional advice. If legal advice or other expert assistance is required, the services of a competent professional person should be sought.

— From a *Declaration of Principles* jointly adopted by a Committee of the American Bar Association and a Committee of Publishers and Associations.

This book is available at quantity discounts for bulk purchases.
For information, call 1-800-872-5627.

Visit our exciting small business Web site at www.businesstown.com

WELLER PRODUCTIONS LOGOS

Within the first five pages, Dan Kennedy had me taking notes. By the end of the book I had devised an entirely new strategy for my video marketing company. Every businessperson needs this book and will find example after example of techniques to enrich their product or service.

Great ideas, proven success in a step-by-step fashion . . . that's what you need for your company's continued growth, and that's what you'll get from Dan Kennedy's book: *The Ultimate Marketing Plan.*

—ROBB WELLER
President, Weller Productions
Television and Radio Personality
(Has hosted: *Entertainment Tonight,*
The Home Show, and *Win, Lose or Draw*)

The author, Dan Kennedy, is available for a limited number of speaking engagements and consulting assignments. He also has a selection of audiocassettes and newsletters on business topics available. For information, fax: Dan Kennedy, at (602) 269-3113, or visit his Web site at *www.dankennedy.com*

CONTENTS

PREFACE

On airplanes, at cocktail parties, I'm always confused when I'm asked what I do. I spend some of my time as a "professional speaker," running around the country getting paid to talk—mostly about the subject of this book, *The Ultimate Marketing Plan*, and its predecessor-companion book, *The Ultimate Sales Letter*. But I've pretty much given up identifying myself as a "speaker." A lot of people think that's a stereo component, and they start asking me questions about CDs and such.

Often I say I'm a marketing consultant, which I am more than anything else. At a party, one lady who overheard that rushed over. "Really? A marketing consultant? Good. For years I've been wondering and have never had anybody to ask—why does every damned shopping cart have one bad wheel?"

Well, what is "marketing," anyway?

My basic definition is that it is getting the right message to the right people via the right media and methods.

The purpose of this book is to equip you with the same process I use as a consultant in helping clients craft the right message for their products, services, or businesses, choose the best media and methods to deliver it, and choose the best prospects to deliver it to.

The last section of this book gives you a fill-in-the-blank Ultimate Marketing Plan for your use. Personally, I detest planning. I've got the classic entrepreneurial nature—"Ready? FIRE! Aim." So if you start wondering about this book . . . if you start muttering, "Plan? Geez. Let's just go sell something," well, I understand. However, here's my promise to you: if you will honestly take the time to go through this book from start to finish without skimming or skipping, think about what you read, and then sit down in a quiet place and fill in the Plan's Think-Sheets, you *will* be more effective, efficient, and successful in whatever business you're in.

Each day, the average American consumer watches about four hours of television and is bombarded by about 100 commercials. That same consumer hears 35 radio commercials each day, sees 202 newspaper ads each day, and receives three to 10 direct-mail solicitations each day. This doesn't even take into account telemarketing, newspaper inserts, magazines, and so forth. And some demographic groups receive even more advertising messages than others.

The "business customer" gets the same barrage as every other consumer plus ads in trade journals and business magazines and a lot more direct mail.

There are a lot of folks out there competing with you for your customers' and prospects' attention, interest, and dollars. To win in this kind of tough, intensely competitive environment, you need the *ultimate* marketing plan. With this book as your consultant, you can create one for your product, service, or business.

—Dan Kennedy

1

PUTTING TOGETHER THE RIGHT MESSAGE

In 1978, when I started my career as a professional speaker and seminar leader, one of the venerable deans of public speaking, Cavett Robert, sagely cautioned: "Don't be in too much of a hurry to promote, until you get good. Otherwise you just speed up the rate at which the world finds out you're no good." Harsh but good advice. It's been my observation since that large numbers of businesspeople in all fields rush to promote without stopping long enough to be sure they have something really worth promoting.

A different expression of this same idea is this anonymous poem for advertisers:

A lion met a tiger
As they drank beside a pool
Said the tiger, "Tell me why
You're roaring like a fool."

"That's not foolish," said the lion
With a twinkle in his eyes
"They call me king of all the beasts
Because I advertise!"

A rabbit heard them talking
And ran home like a streak
He thought he'd try the lion's plan,
But his roar was just a squeak.

A fox came to investigate—
Had luncheon in the woods.
Moral: when you advertise, my friends,
Be sure you've got the goods!

Marketing—and *The Ultimate Marketing Plan*—begins not with any particular media or strategy; it starts with putting together the best, most promotable message possible that truthfully represents "the goods" you've got.

I'm going to suggest a little exercise to you. Stop reading here long enough to get your Yellow Pages telephone directory out and open it up to the business category your present or planned business best fits in. Start with the first ad and a thick pad of paper. Write down each promise, feature, benefit, and statement in the first advertiser's ad. When you find one of these same statements in the next advertiser's ad, just put a mark next to it, and keep stick-counting the number of times the same statement appears in all the ads in the section. If you find a new or different statement in any of the ads, add it to your list, then stick-count the number of times it reoccurs in other ads.

This exercise is instructive for two reasons. First, the Yellow Pages is the most competitive, toughest advertising arena there is. With most other media, your ad is not surrounded by your competitors' ads. Your billboard stands alone. Your sales letter or brochure, in the recipient's hands, has exclusive if momentary attention. But in the Yellow Pages, your ad is next to, above, below, and/or grouped with all your competitors' ads. You are all presenting your messages simultaneously to the same prospective customer. Here, only the strong survive; only the strongest prosper.

Second, in spite of this obvious, extreme competitiveness, your stick-counted list will glaringly reveal one astounding fact: Everybody is saying the same thing. Everybody is delivering the same message.

While this seems to be the way to do things, because that's the way everybody is doing things, it is definitely the wrong approach if you seek exceptional success, even dominance in your marketplace.

Contrary to all this me-tooism, the "key to the vault" in marketing in general and in this tough medium in particular is a message that differentiates you from all your competitors in a positive, appealing, preferably compelling way. Many marketing pros call this a "Unique Selling Proposition."

ULTIMATE MARKETING SECRET WEAPON #1
THE GREAT USP

A *Unique Selling Proposition* (USP) is a way of explaining your position against your competition. When a supermarket chain labels itself as "THE Low Price Leader," it has made a positioning promise.

It's also a way of summarizing and telegraphing one of the chief benefits, often the chief benefit of the business, product, or service being marketed. When I first wrote this book, Chrysler was making much out of being the only American carmaker to include driver's-side air bags as standard equipment. At the time that worked for them as a USP; today, the competition has caught up, and Chrysler is presumably in search of a new way to leap ahead of their competitors and stand apart in a crowded marketplace.

Your USP may express the "theme" of your business, product, or service. Think: which coffee is "mountain grown"? Which beer is made with "the cold, clear water of the Rockies"?

These examples show that a USP can be based on just about anything: price, product ingredient, positioning. There are USPs based on color, size, scent, celebrity endorsement, location, hours of operation, and on and on.

As you concentrate on developing a new USP for your enterprise, you'll be newly aware of the USPs of other businesses, and you can learn from their examples. To hone your marketing mind, you need to become USP-sensitive and ask these questions about every business, product, and service you encounter in your daily activities:

1. Does this business have a USP?
2. If not, can I think of one for it?
3. If so, is there a way I can think of to improve it?
4. Is there any idea here I can "steal" for my use?

HOW A TERRIFIC USP BUILT AN ENTREPRENEURIAL EMPIRE

Some years ago, two brothers determined they would put themselves through college by running a small business. Early on, the business was unsuccessful, and one brother bailed out on the other. The brother left with the business eventually came up with a USP that made him a multimillionaire and revolutionized his industry.

His USP? "Fresh, hot pizza delivered in 30 minutes or less, guaranteed." I don't need to tell you the name of his company. In fact, I did a little word-association survey with 50 people, asking them to say the first word that popped into their minds when I said, "pizza." Of the 50, 41 replied, "Domino's." That's almost 85 percent.

Question: if we went out into your marketplace and asked 100 or 1,000 people to play the game, gave them the generic name for your type of business, and 85 percent of them responded by naming you, how well would you be doing?

I had the privilege of interviewing Tom Monaghan for a magazine article some years ago, and there's no doubt that his success and that of his company is linked to a complex list of factors, notably including his personal success philosophy and his ability to instill it in his franchisees. But there's also no doubt that his USP is largely responsible for the rapid rise and dominance of his company in the pizza industry. It generated enough wealth to let Tom indulge his lifelong fantasy of buying the Detroit Tigers, with a $53 million-dollar price tag, collect classic cars, give most generously to his church and favorite charities, and be financially independent and secure at a relatively young age.

That is the power of a truly great USP. It *is* worth working on the invention of a strong USP for your product, service, or business. And it's not necessarily easy. I know clients who've taken months, even years, to finally hit on a USP that they liked and that really worked. For each, the months of frustrating brain strain have paid off handsomely.

A list of "Idea Starters" for USPs appears at the end of this chapter. Another good source of ideas is the public library. There, for free, you can wander through Yellow Page directories and newspapers from cities all across the country as well as hundreds of consumer, business, trade, and specialty magazines. Another source of ideas is the Internet: roam cyberspace in the comfort of home, visit Web sites in and outside your business category, in search of inspiring USP ideas. Then you can boldly go where few others go, into the marketplace with a really exciting USP of your own!

PRODUCTS THAT HAVE USP POWER

The Christmas shopping season always brings forth a crop of interesting new kitchen appliances—one recent year it was the

Iced Tea Pot. When I first saw this advertised, I burst out laughing. Its manufacturer, the Mr. Coffee Company, is laughing all the way to the bank. Imagine: we can no longer make iced tea in any old kettle; we must have the precisely correct Iced Tea Pot.

It reminds me of a funny phenomenon we have here in the Southwest: the Sun Tea Jar. Because we have searing sunshine every day, it's easy to sun-brew tea just by putting a large jar of water outside for a few hours with tea bags in it. Obviously, any old glass jar will do the job. But on store shelves you'll find large glass jars with the words "Sun Tea Jar" silkscreened on them for sale at four or five times what unmarked jars in the next aisle sell for. And you'll find people cheerfully buying them. After all, what kind of goofball would brew sun tea in a pickle jar?

Some years back, I was president of a fairly large manufacturing company with its own in-house print shop. One day I noticed how much paper was going to waste in the shop and brilliantly decreed that the waste be kept and made into pads for the office staff to jot phone messages on, thus eliminating the need to buy those square pads of pink paper imprinted "Phone Message" from the office-supply store. Why, I reasoned, should we buy little pads of paper at retail when we're already buying large truckloads of paper at wholesale?

I almost had a mutiny on my hands. Pointing to the odd-colored, odd-sized pads we got free from our own print shop, the secretaries said, "Those are scratch pads." Holding up the pink imprinted pads from the office-supply store, they said, "These are phone-message pads." End of discussion.

Purely through customized or proprietary appearance, these products have taken on USP POWER that is almost invincible.

If you really want to see this at work, visit an athletic-shoe store. I'm not much of a casual dresser, but, immediately before a day of walking at Disney World, I decided it would be smart to get some comfortable "sneaks." Forty minutes and eighty-five bucks later, I left the store with a thorough education: there are shoes for walking on pavement, for walking on grass, for walking a lot, for walking a little, for jogging, for tennis, basketball, soccer, football, baseball, trampolining, with pumps, without pumps—but there are no more "sneaks."

Consider these products with USP POWER:

- Microwave dinners for kids to make for themselves
- Clarion Cosmetics' "computer" that tells you what colors are right for you
- Luzianne iced tea bags
- A stress management seminar for career women
- A shampoo and conditioner for "swimmer's hair"

And watch the TV commercials for the appetite suppressant products: there's one for people with the urge to binge late in the day, another for people who need help all day, and yet another "extra strength" one—presumably for people with not even a smidgen of willpower.

It's even possible for a mundane product to get USP POWER purely from its package. In 1991, when I wrote the first edition of this book, McDonald's did just that for the cheeseburger with its McDLTs hot-side-stays-hot, cold-side-stays-cold, two-bin styrofoam container. More recently, Yuban did it with premeasured filter packs for automatic coffee makers so you don't have to count out scoops. Very recently, the cereal companies have put pre-measured, single servings of cereal and milk in side by side "pockets" of a plastic container stored in the refrigerator.

TO THE PROSPECTIVE CUSTOMER'S QUESTION, YOUR USP IS THE ANSWER

When you set out to attract a new, prospective customer to your business for the first time, there is one, paramount question you must answer:

> *"Why should I choose your business/product/service*
> *versus any/every other competitive option*
> *available to me?"*

I invented this question to help businesspeople "get" USP, and to use as a crowbar to pry ideas out of their heads, to dig out the makings of a good USP. If you can't answer the question, you won't get a USP, but you also have bigger problems—typically it'll mean that you've been getting your customers only because of cheapest price, convenient location, your personal smile-n-shoeshine charisma, or the good fortune of being the only provider, and all these leave you very, very vulnerable to new competition. You need a USP.

I choose Domino's pizza because it's gonna get to me hot, fast. I chose the McDLT because my lettuce and tomato stayed cool and crisp. (I miss the McDLT.) I chose Yuban so I didn't have to count scoops. I choose Minit-Lube because I hate hanging around greasy, dirty gas-station waiting areas. Why do I choose the chiropractor I go to? The restaurants I regularly patronize? The dealership where I buy my cars? More often than not, it's because each has USP POWER that appeals to me.

BOOSTING USP POWER
WITH AN IRRESISTIBLE OFFER

I grew up in Ohio and briefly owned an ad agency in a rural community halfway between Cleveland and Akron. At least a dozen times each winter there was enough snow and ice on the country roads to make it ill-advised if not downright impossible to go anywhere. Those days the office stayed closed and I stayed stuck at home.

On one such day, in the midst of a severe blizzard, I stared out my apartment window and watched a neighbor slog through the snow, struggle through the wind, scrape ice from his car's windshield, unfreeze the car's door latch with a cigarette lighter, fight to start the car, and finally slip and slide off into the storm. "I wonder," I asked myself, "what would motivate a guy to go out in weather like this?"

Then I remembered a very similar storm just a couple of winters before when I had quite literally risked my life and badly banged up my car driving all the way from Akron, Ohio to Murray State University in Kentucky to spend a weekend with my girlfriend of that time. For hours, it snowed so hard I honestly couldn't see past the hood ornament of my car. Every bridge was so icy I spun my way across it. Yet I pressed on.

Waiting for me in Murray, Kentucky was "an irresistible offer!"

If you can come up with an offer that irresistible, you are really on to something! Try this one on for size: for $198 per person, $396 per couple, I'll put you up in a luxurious minisuite in an exciting Las Vegas hotel, right on the famous strip . . . give you tickets to a show with name entertainers . . . put a chilled bottle of champagne in your room . . . let you drink as much of whatever you want whether you're at the gaming tables, playing the slots, or in one of the lounges . . . hand you $1,000 of my money to gamble with . . . let you keep all your winnings . . . and, as a bonus, guarantee you'll at least win either a color TV, a VCR, or a faux-diamond ring. Obviously I'm not going to give this incredible deal to everybody in the whole world. There can only be x (a small number) of these vacation packages available, first come, first served, and the race is on. Assuming you trust the offer, how fast can you get to a phone and call in to reserve yours? Would you go out in a blizzard and drive to the post office to get your order form in the mail before the deadline?

Well, this was a real offer, from Mr. Bob Stupak, the sole, entrepreneurial owner of the original Vegas World Hotel and one of the savviest marketers I know ever to take on Las Vegas. For years, Bob kept his hotel filled to capacity, kept a waiting list going, and got paid months, even years in advance by his guests—all thanks to his invention of this irresistible offer. He used the cash flow generated by selling that "package" to grow his hotel from a tiny, slots only joint to a huge, two-towered showplace. A few years ago, he sold his interest to a bigger corporation, and Vegas World became the Stratosphere, the Stupak-style marketing ended, and financial troubles multiplied like rabbits in spring.

The Embassy Suites hotel chain has flourished for years and sparked much competition thanks to its offer of "every room a suite," free evening cocktails, and free breakfast. For many years, the Howard Johnson's restaurants were famous for their Friday night all-you-can-eat clam fries.

One of the mail-order catalog companies I occasionally buy from recently sent me a "preferred customer catalog" from which I could buy anything I wanted with "no payments for six months." I confess—I went through that darned catalog looking for something to buy!

One of the classic, often-used irresistible offers is the book and record clubs' "Choose 6 for 10¢," like the offer shown in Fig. 1.

FIGURE 1

In the marketing of my own newsletter, I utilized a "knock-off" of this premise for several years, inviting new subscribers to choose any six Special Reports as the free bonus with their subscription. Today, I beat that offer's performance with an even more generous irresistible offer, or, what we call a "bribe offer; shown here in Fig. 2—the first page of the whole letter making the offer. If you want to see the entire offer, you can go to my Web site at *www.dankennedy.com* or fax a request to (602) 269-3113, and I'll send it to you.

BEING IN THE RIGHT PLACE AT THE RIGHT TIME WITH THE RIGHT USP

I recently listened to a client, Ned Allen, President of Florida Communities and Intercoastal Communities, two retirement-community firms, reminisce about his starting the famous Steak 'N' Ale restaurants smack in the middle of a national recession. He had started the first restaurant with just $2,000, made it successful, and committed to the construction and opening of seven new restaurants just as the recession hit.

Ned says: "We had to quickly change our thinking to match the timing we had to work with. We developed new, lower-cost, higher-perceived-value menu items, and by offering the look, feel, atmosphere and taste of a gourmet steakhouse at a surprisingly low price, we had the right product at just the right time."

As I was writing first edition of this book, Ned was not alone in predicting another three- to four-year-long recession, and he was again busy creating just the right product for it; in this case, a new type of a manufactured home for his companies' communities—this one with several hundred square feet less than any other home and, therefore, a substantially lower cost, but an

I want to give you the tapes of my latest
Marketing & Moneymaking SuperConference,
which people paid $2,487.00 each to attend,
free.

FREE:

6 Audio Tapes, 5 Special Reports, 1 Book, 2 Critique Certificates, Telephone Consulting & Coaching, a veritable truckload of moneymaking information and assistance.......ALL FREE........ and all you have to do to get all of it is say "maybe."

Have I finally lost my mind?

Dear Friend,

   Although you have purchased my books or tapes or attended one of my seminars in the past, and although we have previously invited you to subscribe to my NO B.S. MARKETING LETTER, it has been brought to my attention that you are NOT getting my monthly Letter (full to the brim with advice that directly boosts your income, fast) --- and I can<u>not</u> allow that situation to continue, so.....

I am going to bury you in "bribes", just to get you to test-drive my Marketing Letter.

   Listen to this: <u>all you have to do is say "*maybe* "</u>............try 3 Issues of my Letter. If that doesn't hook you for life; if you can't see the profit from continuing, you can change your "maybe" to an emphatic "no", and get a full refund plus ten bucks for your trouble. (Details later in this letter.)

   Now, let's take a look at the pick-up truck load of "stuff" I have piled up, ready to rush to your doorstep - FREE! - "stuff" that will stimulate your marketing-mind, grease your greed glands, electrify your enthusiasm, <u>point you to overlooked opportunities</u> in your business, <u>hand you ready-to-use and incredibly powerful strategies</u> for magnetically attracting lots of new customers or clients..........selling more, more often to current customers.........one way or another, <u>creating a FLOOD OF MONEY</u> rushing toward YOUR door.

FIGURE 2

interior design that made it seem much, much bigger than it was and that had lots of nifty "gingerbread" touches that added to its perceived value.

Ned turned his $2,000 investment in Steak 'N' Ale into over $5 million when he sold out to Green Giant Foods. He's since made another fortune with his new "Land Yacht" mini-retirement home and his inventive approach to low-cost retirement living in Florida.

Of course, it's no secret that timing is a business success factor. But matching a USP with the right timing can dramatically multiply success.

HOW "MARKETING BY VALUES" STRENGTHENS YOUR MESSAGE

One of my first mentors in business often said: "If you stand for nothing, you'll fall for anything." Just about anything—recession, new competition—can topple a business devoid of values.

Although there are many great success stories in the fast-food industry, none stand above McDonald's. The McDonald's empire was built on Ray Kroc's unwavering, some would say fanatical, commitment to *consistency*—the idea that the food items at a McDonald's in Iowa are identical to those found under the arches in California. Try to find anything close to this kind of consistency in any other national restaurant chain.

In my opinion, the Holiday Inn chain has lost all touch with its founders' values, but back when I started hitting the road as a frequent business traveler I preferred Holiday Inns for that same reason—consistency. Kemmons Wilson was determined that travelers could depend—DEPEND—on Holiday Inns for the basics: clean rooms, safety, courteous service.

Federal Express invented, built, and dominated an industry because of a commitment to on-time, as-promised delivery, and there are many classic stories of FedEx employees going to extraordinary extremes to keep faith with this fundamental value.

I would suggest, incidentally, that a clearly defined quality appropriate to your business be one of your values. *In Search of Excellence* author Tom Peters jokes about the retail executive who became aggravated at Peters' criticism of his business in a seminar and cried out: "We are no worse than anybody else!" Tom Peters had a graphic artist design a company logo with that slogan in it: We are no worse than anybody else. Unfortunately, many business leaders settle for just this approach.

Most small-business people grumble when I recommend reading Tom Peters, complaining that his stuff is for big business, not them. And I've just used three big businesses as examples myself, but I believe they became big because of their code of values, and any business of any size can learn from their commitments.

A client and friend of mine, Don Dwyer, now passed away, built a huge international franchisor organization, encompassing over 2,000 franchisees in three service industries, from scratch, in just a handful of years—thanks, in a large degree, to his early development of, adherence to, and enthusiastic teaching of a very strong code of values. It goes like this:

1. We believe in superior service to our customers, to our community, and to each other as members of the business community.
2. We believe that if we count our blessings every day, we will keep the negatives away.

3. We believe success is the result of clear, cooperative positive thinking.

4. We believe that in order to build our business we must re-earn our positions every day by excelling in every way.

5. We believe that management should seek out what employees are doing right and treat every associate in a friendly, fair, frank, and firm way.

6. We believe that problems should be welcomed tranquilly and should be used as learning experiences.

7. We believe our Creator put us on this Earth to win. We will keep faith with His wishes by winning honestly and accepting our daily successes humbly, knowing that a higher power has guided us to victory.

8. We believe in the untapped potential of every human being. Every person we help achieve that potential will bring us one step closer to achieving our potential.

9. We believe that loyalty adds consistency to our lives.

10. We believe in building our country through the free-enterprise system. We will demonstrate this belief by constantly attracting people to seek opportunity.

Don did *not* come up with that Code *after* making millions, to have an impressive plaque for his office wall. He developed the Code in the very infancy of his business, when he was operating out of a small garage (with one truck), telling the few people who would listen that he was going to quickly build a $100 million-a-year corporation. (In 1990, he topped $50 million. I'm sure his companies have gone on to get closer and closer to his remarkable, original goal.)

WHAT'S YOUR MAGNIFICENT MISSION?

The nature and details of my business interests have changed quite a bit over the last ten years or so, but I've always kept them linked to this mission: to be responsible for getting how-to-succeed education into the hands of more people than any other individual or enterprise.

At one time I saw the implementation of that mission limited to the mail-order marketing of books, cassettes, and courses. Then it expanded to include speaking and seminars. Then television. Then developing products for other publishers. Then consulting with publishers, direct marketers, even multilevel marketing companies. And, in the last few years, I've probably been responsible for directly selling success education materials to well over a million people, and indirectly exposing many more to the ideas. All of this gives most of my business activity some meaning greater than just getting money into the bank accounts. From that comes, I think, a different, superior level of creativity, inspiration, and persistence.

Many moons ago, one of the much-made-fun-of Merv Griffin "theme shows"—a technique more recently copied by *Geraldo*, *Oprah*, etc.—featured a panel of self-made millionaire entrepreneurs: in this instance, Colonel Sanders of KFC, the inventor of the Lear jet, and several others. Merv asked them: "What was your goal—to make money?"

Each guest answered by describing a mission bigger than just making money. Each had a goal, what *Think and Grow Rich* author Napoleon Hill called "a burning desire." Each wanted to *do* something and to *be* someone.

It's interesting that years later, a fabulously wealthy man by most standards (thanks to the sale of his game-show company), Merv Griffin chose to plunge into new, risky businesses rather than just sitting back and enjoying early retirement. He certainly couldn't have been motivated by money itself.

I'm not necessarily saying that you have to have some hidden, ulterior motive or some saintly charitable motive behind your business activities. And I'm not one who feels any guilt about making large amounts of money. But I do find that the business owner who is at least as enthusiastic about the values and mission and processes of his business as he is about its bank balance does best.

Walt Disney was thrilled when he finally achieved significant financial success, but he was much more committed to his ideals for his theme park than he was to piling up personal wealth. Once, driving home, he noticed an attractive new car in a showroom window and thought to himself: "Gee, I wish I could afford that car." He drove a few more blocks before realizing, "Hey, I *can* afford that car!"

I think you'll find the challenges of successfully crafting and conveying great marketing messages easier and more fun to meet when you are on a magnificent mission!

IT'S TIME TO "ASSEMBLE" YOUR MESSAGE

You have undoubtedly had the "joy" of opening a large box and laying out a hundred parts, pieces, screws, and bolts on the floor and trying to assemble it into the beautiful bookcase or computer work-station or whatever pictured on the outside of the carton. Be honest—how much extra would you pay to get it assembled? (Now there's an idea for a service business: We Put It Together, Inc.)

Well, there you are again, with pieces of a marketing message. Actually, that's where you *start*. Keeping in mind everything we've discussed in this chapter, get a large pile of blank 3"x 5" cards and start putting one fact, feature, benefit, promise, offer component, and idea on each card—until you have, over a series of brain-storming sessions, exhausted everything you know about your business and its competitors. Then do your best to prioritize the items, in order of their probable importance to your customers and their contribution to differentiating you from your competition. Through the exercise, you can come to the creation of the best possible USP, a supporting sales story, and one or more related offers.

PRESENTING YOUR MESSAGE

Regardless of the target markets you later select and the modifications you make in your message to fit these markets, and regardless of the media mix you use to deliver the presentation of your message, there are some key ideas to keep in mind about making the right presentation.

THE BATTLE TO COMMUNICATE

At Stew Leonard's famous super-supermarket,* they were bringing in fresh fish every day, carefully packaging it, and displaying it in their freezer cases, clearly and proudly labeled as FRESH FISH.

They had the right message—people who like fish really like fresh fish. Few other supermarkets go to the trouble and expense of bringing in a lot of fresh fish, so they even had a working USP. They also, incidentally, were getting the right message to the right market; most of Stew Leonard's customers are upscale consumers with the money to buy fresh fish, the time and inclination to prepare a meal with it, and an appreciation for it. Still, something was wrong. It turned out to be a presentation problem.

One of their customers told them that she wished they had *real* fresh fish, like the fish at the wharf-side fish markets: fish lying there on slabs of ice. So Stew Leonard's people divided the fresh fish that came in each day and presented the same fish two different ways: one, as they had been, cleaned up and nicely packaged; two, unpackaged, on a slab of ice, in a little display unit topped with a sign reading: Fresh Fish Market.

---

*Stew Leonard has built what is believed to be the world's largest and most unusual super-market. You can read about it in Tom Peters' book *In Search of Excellence.*

Guess what? Their sales of fresh fish more than doubled. To me, this little story hammers home the idea that it is quite often difficult to communicate successfully.

ULTIMATE MARKETING SECRET WEAPON #2 BEING CLEARLY UNDERSTOOD

Lexus and Infiniti, new top-luxury cars, were introduced to the market at about the same time, and as Lexus overwhelmingly outsold Infiniti, Infiniti dealers begged the company and its ad agency to "show 'em the car" in the TV commercials. Instead, the company insisted on a Zen-ish, Twin Peaks-ish series of elegant commercials that never showed the car. A bold experiment, but a bad idea nevertheless.

There *are* notable examples of outrageously clever, intensely creative, excitingly innovative marketing campaigns that have worked well, but if you prefer to put the odds in your favor, you'll pass on this high risk, longshot approach and always opt for being clearly understood.

One of the most interesting failure phenomena in advertising is the development of an idea, character, or presentation that is tremendously memorable in itself yet fails to sell the products it represents. Everybody knows about the funny pink bunny with the drum in the battery commercials—but do you know the brand of battery he represents? Surveys show over half name the company's competitor! And over the last five years, while showing off the bunny every way imaginable, that company's market share has declined, not improved.

The confused consumer either does not buy or sometimes buys the wrong product! Bottom line: bend over backward to avoid confusing your customer.

PRESENTATION KEY #1: BE WELL ORGANIZED

The customer has to be led up five steps to a buying or action decision—to return an order form, redeem a coupon, call for an appointment, come into a store, or buy a product or service—and the five steps are the same for any and every product or service, for marketing to consumers or business-to-business:

STEP 1: AWARENESS OF NEED AND/OR DESIRE
STEP 2: PICKING THE "THING" THAT FULFILLS THE
         NEED/DESIRE
STEP 3: PICKING THE SOURCE FOR THE THING
STEP 4: ACCEPTING THE SOURCE'S PRICE
STEP 5: FINDING REASONS TO ACT NOW

Sometimes you have to start your presentation at Step 1; other times you get to start on Step 2. A company selling dog food gets to start on Step 2; a company selling dog vitamins has to start on Step 1.

Go back to the Yellow Pages and again turn to the ads in your section. Look at several of them carefully, and ask yourself whether or not, from the top, the headline on down, these ads present their messages according to the organized structure above.

I think you'll agree with me—most do not. Believe me, this *is* a big mistake. Every presentation of a marketing message via any and every medium should adhere to a safe, proven, effective structure.

Let me give you a couple of great examples of this structure in action:

Example #1

I just decided to buy a portable fireplace that burns some chemical "logs," gives off heat, glows, replicates the look and the fragrance of a wood fire, but needs no chimney, is safe, and can be moved from the living room to the bedroom with ease. Before I saw this thing in the Hammacher-Schlemmer catalog, I didn't even know such a thing existed or that I needed or wanted one. However, seeing it reminded me that in moving recently from one house to another, we'd given up a fireplace. I couldn't care less, but my wife really enjoyed the fireplace. (Yes—in Phoenix.) So, I instantly became aware of a desire to own a fireplace, in this case, to make my wife happy. I was on Step 1.

I am not about to move to a home with a fireplace, and the home we now live in, which I love, is not conducive in its design for a built-in, conventional fireplace, nor do I want to incur the expense and bother of having one built. The idea of a portable fireplace is pretty appealing. Okay, up to Step 2.

Now I want one. Where to get it? I've never seen one anywhere but in this company's catalog. They make it very easy to get—a toll-free call. They'll gift-wrap the darned thing, so I can give it to my wife as a present. They'll deliver it to my door. And they guarantee I'll be happy with it. Bingo. Step 3.

In this case, Step 4's virtually a must issue as my thinking has precluded comparison shopping. (By the way, this thing costs $499.)

Standing on Step 4, though, the sale breaks down. It's only August, and the next gift-giving occasion is Christmas, so I put the catalog in a pile of stuff to look at later in the year, when I start doing my holiday shopping. They needed to give me a reason, an incentive or a reward, for ordering immediately.

Example #2

I do a considerable amount of consulting work within the chiropractic profession, helping practitioners learn to market their services effectively. I consider the members of this profession my friends, but I must tell you that they remain stubbornly lousy at marketing. Most of them deviate from this organized structure in most of the media they use, yet they need to follow these five steps as badly as any marketer I can think of.

For them, Step 1 has to be creating awareness of the need or the desire: reminding people that they do suffer chronically from, say, headaches or low back pain or neck stiffness, that they consume frightening quantities of pills, drugs, and alcohol to mute the symptoms, and that deep down inside they desire optimum health and fitness. Chiropractors *cannot* afford to assume that the public is instantly, automatically interested in this.

ULTIMATE MARKETING SECRET WEAPON #3 CAREFULLY AND THOROUGHLY ELIMINATE ALL ASSUMPTIONS

Step 2, then, and only then, is to present chiropractic as a viable, effective, accepted, credible, safe, gentle, nonsurgical, nondrug alternative treatment for various problems and ailments. Step 3, only after Steps 1 and 2, is the individual chiropractor presenting his USP-empowered marketing message and offer.

Step 4, then, is handling the issues of fees, costs, and affordability. Here we have taught chiropractors to be creative in offering to accept every imaginable insurance plan, handle all the paperwork, accept major credit cards, even offer installment financing services through finance companies.

Step 5, finally, is pushing the prospective patient over the edge, so he or she picks up the phone right now, calls, makes an appointment and keeps it.

Fail to walk the customer up those steps, in that order, and you act at your peril.

PRESENTATION KEY #2: IGNITE INTEREST

Please—I don't care if you are marketing Hostess Twinkies, garden hoses, industrial widgets, or any one of a zillion commodities or services that you and everyone you know has accepted as dull and ordinary and mundane, maybe even trivial—there is a way, and you must find it, to present that message in a truly interesting way.

ULTIMATE MARKETING SIN #1
BEING BORING

Some years back, I did some consulting work for a manufacturer of security cameras and video monitoring devices for retail stores. I'm here to tell you that there's nothing inherently fascinating about this.

Still, I knew that I had to *ignite interest* in the storeowner's mind and heart, intellectually and emotionally. I invented a give-away booklet with this obviously provocative title:

HOW TO STEAL YOUR BOSS BLIND!

Believe me, when a storeowner sees this book, his interest *is* ignited. He eagerly, passionately wants to know what is in the book. Just as an aside, the word "secret" evokes a powerful emotional response in most people. It instantly hits our curiosity button. For some reason, just as cats are bothered by closed doors, we are driven nuts by secrets. We want to know. You can ignite interest easily if you have secrets to divulge.

Consider this: would you be interested, or do you know somebody who would be interested, in knowing a medical doctor's secret for absolutely, 100 percent suppressing hunger so you can diet, even skip meals or fast with no hunger pains, no desire for food? If I told you that this doctor's secret had been tested and proven on 10,000 patients, would that make it even more interesting to you?

If at all possible, you should find ways to add drama to your presentations. I do a lot of script-writing and consulting work in the TV infomercial business—you know, those 30-minute-long commercials that look like TV shows—and I'm very envious of one I had nothing to do with: the old *Amazing Discoveries* show selling car polish, where they set a fire on the hood of the car . . . and poured acid onto it! That show was hugely, fabulously successful, and it is remembered many years after its heyday, because it ignited interest with a dramatic demonstration. Since then, the dramatic demonstration has been a staple in many successful infomercials. When the product can be the star, it's an advantage.

You can make the presentation of your marketing message more interesting in many different ways, some depending on the medium being used, including:

1. Before/after photographs
2. Dramatic stories of satisfied customers
3. Shocking statistics
4. Dramatic slogans, headlines, statements
5. Physical demonstration

PRESENTATION KEY #3: ASK FOR ACTION

Most marketing-message presentations are too wimpy. They stop short of demanding any action. "Here's our beautiful new car"—but they stop short of: get into a showroom this weekend, take a test drive, and take home a free case of Coke just for test driving it. "Here's our wonderful new shampoo"—but they stop short of: now go to your phone, dial our toll-free number, and we'll rush you a free sample and $5.00 in discount coupons.

ULTIMATE MARKETING SECRET WEAPON #4
THE GUTS TO ASK FOR ACTION EVERY TIME, IN EVERY PRESENTATION

Very early in my selling career, I heard Zig Ziglar* say that the difference between being a professional salesperson and a professional visitor is asking for the order. Zig also said: "Timid salespeople have skinny kids." I fortunately accepted this idea and have never, ever been shy about asking for the action. However, most salespeople, even otherwise very good ones, are held back by this hesitancy, hobbled by some strange love of subtlety.

I spent a full week touring one company's real-estate developments, pretending to be a prospective buyer, putting the salespeople through their paces. Almost without exception, all the salespeople did a fine job of establishing rapport, being courteous and friendly, asking smart questions, showing me the communities and the houses. And, almost unanimously, they all stopped way short of asking me to buy.

Four chiropractors joined together and manned a very attractive, professional-appearing booth at a health fair in a busy shopping mall over Labor Day weekend, but wound up with no new patients from their efforts. Care to know why? They never asked anybody to book an exam appointment. They smiled, greeted, handed out literature, gave scoliosis exams, checked blood pressure, and answered questions, but they never asked anybody to take any action.

---

*Zig Ziglar is one of the best-known, most popular motivational speakers and sales trainers in America. His books include *See You at the Top* and *Secrets of Closing the Sale*. For 10 years, Zig, Peter Lowe, and I have been the three speakers appearing at every single SUCCESS EVENT, between 20 and 30 each year, typically addressing audiences of 10,000 to 30,000 people. The Zig Ziglar Corporation is located in Dallas, Texas. Information about the events can be obtained from Peter Lowe International, (800) 989-8990, or my Web site, *www.dankennedy.com.*

Again, check the ads in the Yellow Pages. Also look at the ads in a newspaper or the trade magazine related to your business. Isn't it amazing how many stop short of asking you to take any specific action, or, if they do, offer no really good reason, incentive, or reward for doing as they ask? Wimpy. Wimpy. Wimpy.

TOUCH EVERY BASE EVERY TIME

You don't have to be a baseball fan to know this rule or, if you prefer, tradition: even when the hitter whacks the ball out of the ballpark and into outer space, it's not a home run on the scoreboard until he goes around the bases—and touches every one. In gym-class baseball I was tagged out after hitting a home run and walking the bases but carelessly stepping over second base instead of on it. I've never forgotten that.

The right presentation of the right marketing message touches every base, every time. It assumes nothing. It takes nothing for granted. It strives for clarity and simplicity and even, many times, brevity—but never, ever achieves those things through shortcuts or skipping bases.

3

PICKING THE RIGHT TARGETS

There is an old joke about a wife insisting on joining her husband for the first time on his annual deer-hunting trip. He stations her at the bottom of the hill, instructs her to fire her gun in the air if she sees any deer—which is very unlikely at that location—and he and his buddy stomp off into the woods. Shortly thereafter, they hear shots and run back through the woods and down the hill to find the wife holding a gun on a very unhappy looking fellow. "Okay lady," he says, "it's your deer. Can I at least get my saddle off of it?"

Obviously, no matter how well equipped you are with the best gun, bullets, and other hunting equipment, you still won't do very well aiming at the wrong targets.

ULTIMATE MARKETING SIN #2
WASTING YOUR WEAPONRY AIMING
AT THE WRONG TARGETS

My friend and true marketing guru Gary Halbert* poses this question: if you were going to open a new hamburger stand in town, what is the one thing you would want most? Many people answer: the best hamburgers in town, or a secret sauce, or a great cook, or a commanding name, logo or character, like Ronald McDonald. But Gary's answer is a starving crowd. I agree, and our job in Step Three is to find or develop a starving crowd for your products, services, or business.

---

*Gary Halbert is one of the leading direct-response advertising and direct marketing experts in America. Gary currently publishes *The Gary Halbert Letter* and occasionally conducts advanced marketing seminars, with fees as high as $7,000 per attendee. You can contact Gary at: The Halbert Letter, c/o Cherrywood Publishing, 3101 SW 34th Ave. #905-467, Ocala, FL 34474, Phone (305) 534-7577.

LEARNING THE LESSON

My first introduction to the idea of targeted marketing was so strange that I've never forgotten it, and the more I've learned about the idea, the more I've appreciated that early lesson.

A man with zero training in marketing was running a direct-sales company, selling distributorships for his products at $5,000 each. His system was to send out a fairly expensive direct-mail package, get back inquiries, and turn those over to staff sales-people called "recruiters" who then phoned or visited the prospective distributors and tried to get them to attend a group meeting. As you can see, this process adds up to a sizeable invest-ment in each prospect. And, for a while, he was literally mailing to the White Pages—to everybody and anybody. He knew this was incredibly inefficient, but had no idea how to do it differently. One day, he had what Tom Peters calls "a blinding flash of the obvious"; he noticed that a huge majority of his successful distrib-utors had crew cuts. This was in the late sixties and crew cuts were supposedly "out." But *his* guys with crew cuts were stubborn indi-vidualists, about forty years old, living in small towns, and working in blue-collar jobs—truck drivers, policemen, high school coaches.

He sent his recruiters out to barber shops all over the state and bought the names, addresses, and telephone numbers of their customers with crew cuts! His success rate with these grade-A prospects was phenomenal.

When he first told me about this, about 20 years ago, I laughed at him. The whole thing sounded ridiculous to me. Maybe it just did to you, too. But now, with 20/20 hindsight, I can tell you that he had stumbled on to the essence of brilliant mar-keting. He had found one of the three means of picking the right targets: demographics.

THIS IS FOR YOU, TOO

Every product, *every* service, *every* business either appeals or has the potential to appeal much more strongly to a certain definable group of people than it appeals to all people, yet most marketers get to their grade-A prospects only by lucky accident—by throwing out their message to everybody and letting the right people find it. This is like getting a message to your aunt in Pittsburgh by dropping 100,000 copies of your letter out of an airplane as you fly over Pennsylvania. I call this "blind archery." Blindfolded, given an unlimited supply of arrows and some degree of luck, you'll hit the target eventually. And you will hit it once out of every *x* times you shoot off an arrow. Of course you'll also hit innocent bystanders, bushes, fenceposts, stray animals, and everything else around.

And arrows are one thing. Dollars are another. Nobody has an unlimited supply of dollars to play with.

You *must* make the commitment to market smarter by picking better targets. Don't say "That's o.k. for somebody else, but it won't work for my business because . . . ." Don't waste your energy figuring out why this can't be done in your business. Any idiot can come up with that list. You need to find the way it can work for you.

A FEW EXAMPLES OF TARGETED MARKETING IN ACTION

Example #1

A fellow in the carpet-cleaning business told me that direct mail never paid off for him. When we investigated the area he had mailed to, we found a very high percentage of renters. Over 70 percent were tenants, not homeowners. "How'd you pick this area anyway?"

"It was the same zip code as my office," he answered.

"Ever drive it, like you were shopping for a home?"

"Nope," he admitted.

"Let's go," I said, and off we went, driving up and down about thirty streets in the area for a couple of hours. We saw many homes in desperate need of repair or paint, poorly maintained lawns, and cars in the driveways and carports five years old or older, some up on jacks being fixed.

"Based on what we've seen outside, who would you expect to see inside these houses?" I asked. 'Nuff said.

The antidote to this direct mail failure was not fixing the literature; it was simply selecting a better target. The carpet-cleaning guy spent the next few days driving the neighborhoods in various zip codes surrounding his office until he found one where the homes shouted: pride of ownership.

In the first area, his mailing had pulled less than one-fourth of one percent in response. Mailing to residents in the new area, the same mailing pulled over 2½ percent.

Example #2

Several years ago, a Sansabelt clothing store opened in a major mall here in Phoenix. Sansabelt features pants with the tab front—no belt—and a hidden elastic waist-band that us chubby guys find helpful.

Most Sansabelt merchandise is sold in department stores and, as a customer, I've always found the selection poor and usually had to trek through several stores to find what I wanted. So I was thrilled at the prospect of a whole store filled with everything Sansabelt makes in every imaginable size and color.

After my first visit, though, I knew the store was doomed. I bet the manager he'd close within six months. He didn't hang around to pay off the bet.

Here's what went wrong. The mall they chose was the biggest center-of-the-city mall. Most of its shoppers are young to the young side of middle age. Yuppies. The majority of Sansabelt customers are middle-aged and up, and at least slightly overweight. Many are retired. Many others are businessmen.

Now there is a mall right smack in the middle of the middle-aged, moneyed folks, near Sun City—the retire-ment capital—and there's one in Mormon-dominated Mesa, Arizona, where there are probably more well-fed, happily overweight guys than anywhere in the world. They could have put a store in each of these malls for what it cost to be in the one they chose, and they'd have been much better located for their target markets.

Then they compounded the problem. Again, a great many loyal Sansabelt customers are overweight busi-nessmen nearing middle age. I went in as they would to buy a couple of Sansabelt suits, prepared to drop about

$700. "We don't stock the suits," I was told, "just the sportswear." Like bright red or yellow golf slacks, at least 20 miles away from the nearest golf course.

If for some reason I wasn't going to stock all the Sansabelt stuff in a Sansabelt store, and I were in that location, if anything I'd stock the suits and forego the golf slacks.

Example #3

Where did Tom Monaghan open up his early Domino's Pizza locations? In college towns, near college campuses. Why? Who do you know who eats more pizza, more often than college kids? Also, at the time, smoking the funny weed was still immensely popular among college kids and, in case you don't know it, "Mary Jane" makes people very, very, very hungry. I have no idea whether or not Tom thought through that, and if he did, I doubt he'd admit it, but he's a bright guy, so you decide for yourself. The point is that, quite literally, he found a starving crowd.

THE THREE BEST WAYS TO TARGET-MARKET

First and most commonly used is geographic targeting, just like my friend in the carpet-cleaning business did. Most businesses that need their customers to come to their store or office or that need to schedule appointments and send salespeople out obviously need to restrict the geography of their marketing. They advertise only in the local newspaper or shopper, use coupon decks mailed to their own or adjacent zip codes, and direct-mail to those same zips.

There's nothing wrong and many things right with this. If you've never read Russell Conwell's classic book *Acres of Diamonds* or heard Earl Nightingale's great recorded message, "Greener Pastures," you should; you'll gain new appreciation for the "value" awaiting discovery right in your own backyard.

However, I suggest keeping two things in mind when you are going to select your target markets via geographical considerations:

First, make sure that the apparent nature of the people living there works for you. This is a cheap (in fact free) and very simplistic look at demographics, but it is nonetheless effective. Do what my carpet-cleaning entrepreneur and I did: drive the neighborhoods. Look around and get a "feel" for the people who live there. You can tell a lot just by driving around. What does the condition of the homes and yards tell you? What kinds of cars predominate? If compacts and sporty cars, young marrieds. If big, bulky sedans and luxury cars, middle aged. If you see BMWs and the like, Yuppies. Do you see a lot of tricycles and skateboards, a lot of basketball backboards on the garages?

You may very well be able to choose preferable neighborhoods or zip code areas this way. You may also discover things that will cause you to modify your themes, copy, and offers.

My second tip is, once you find a geographic target market that works for you, work it to death. Dominate it. People in the real estate business use the term "farming." When a real-estate agent farms an area, he strives to become its best known and loved agent. He mails to every homeowner in the area, goes around door-to-door and introduces himself, distributes a monthly newsletter, sends holiday greeting cards, even gets creatively involved with the community: driving through and giving away free pumpkins at Halloween, sponsoring a neighborhood block party and swap meet, and so on. It's a lot of work, but it's smart work.

There's no reason any retail or service business can't follow this example. If I had a florist shop, a restaurant, or a car wash, I could do exactly the same thing in a targeted residential or business neighborhood. I could frequently mail to everybody. I could take an hour each day and go out and personally introduce myself to the neighbors. I could send holiday greetings. I could throw a party. I could lead a charitable effort in the area for the MDA or some other worthwhile group.

A second selection method has to do with demographics. Demographics are the statistical, behavioral, and even psychological things given groups of people have in common. Demographic selection can be as simple as targeting a preferred age group or as complex as targeting women age 35 to 45 who have careers, read both *Working Woman* and *Cosmopolitan*, carry the American Express card, travel by air at least three times a year, and buy clothes by mail order.

Every medium has and can provide detailed demographic information about its readers, listeners, viewers, or customers. While some media's data are more reliable than others, most are pretty accurate—the media need this same data to make good editorial, programming, or product selections. You can and should take this information very seriously when making media decisions.

If you're renting mailing lists, the same kind of data is available for most lists. More significantly, you can "merge-purge" two or more lists together to get exactly the prospective customers you want. A good list broker can help. It can be quite costly to do sophisticated merge-purges, but even so it's usually a bargain compared to the costly waste of playing "blind archery" with direct mail.

Think again about my friend in the carpet-cleaning business. After choosing one or several zip-code areas based on his drive-by observations, he could get even pickier. He might make the logical assumption that people in certain income brackets are better prospects than others. Folks with household incomes of, say, less than $30,000 a year might find money tight and choose to go through the agony of shampooing their own carpets to save money.

Since he accepts VISA and MasterCard, he might prefer to mail only to people who have those credit cards. And, since families get their carpets dirtier more often, he might want to skip mailing to single people.

So he sits down with his list broker and says: "In these zips, I want married homeowners with kids, with household income of $30,000 and up, who have MasterCards or VISA cards." Using lists derived from the census, credit card holder lists, property ownership records, and other readily available sources, the broker can deliver that exact list.

Incidentally, it can be helpful to collect demographic data about your present customers. If you find certain biases or commonalties in your present customers, you may be able to use them in your criteria for future targeting.

The third way to target market is by affinity or association. I like this approach and use it a great deal for myself and my clients.

Let me give you a personal example: I've been a member of the National Speakers Association, one of two trade associations for lecturers and seminar leaders, since 1978. I have gone out of my way to be visible in the association, through a variety of means, and I'd guess my "name recognition" hits about 70 to 80 percent of the total membership, about 4,000 people. These 4,000 people and I have much in common: first, obviously, I know them and, more important, they know me. I can call attention to our affinity by addressing them as "colleagues" and "fellow members." We share the same business activities, experiences, concerns, and problems. Because I am a known, respected success in this business, the members are interested in what I have to say and in whatever I recommend.

In approximately 20 years, I have sold literally millions of dollars of goods and services to this very small market. In some years, as much as one-third of my income has been derived from this very small market. I am occasionally able to reap pure passive income simply from licensing my endorsement of someone else's product or service being offered to this very small market.

Geographically, these people are scattered all over the United States, Canada, and several foreign countries. Demographically, they have few, if any, dominant commonalties. They are men, women, young, old, fat, thin, conservative, liberal, rich, poor, married, single, with families, without families. But they are still a perfect target market for me purely because of our mutual association. Because of affinity.

As evidence of how well affinity works for me in this case, just as I was doing all the revisions and updating this work, I was in the midst of a direct-mail campaign to this list for a new product, and I'm delighted to report over $226,400 in sales, again from just 4,000 people.

Many other businesspeople can apply this same principle to the trade or professional associations they belong to or to the Chamber of Commerce, Toastmasters, Jaycees, other business and civic groups, church groups, PTAs—whatever they belong to.

I encourage chiropractors and dentists I consult with, for example, to get out of their offices at least eight hours a week to join and actively participate in a number of these associative target markets. Then, instead of advertising to a neighborhood, they can advertise to their fellow members. Instead of farming a community, they can farm a fraternity.

ULTIMATE MARKETING SECRET WEAPON #5
TAILORING AND DELIVERING YOUR MESSAGE
TO THE RIGHT TARGET

I find the pizza wars endlessly interesting. Domino's took the industry by storm by focusing on delivery. Another company has taken a very different tack and is enjoying great success by targeting a very specific demographic group. Pistol Pete's Pizza, with stores in several states here in the Southwest, very clearly aims its products, prices, restaurant environments, and advertising at families.

Each location features a working merry-go-round and lots of other games for the kids. The TV commercials use a happy cowboy character who urges families to c'mon in and have fun. Their pricing is low-end, so the family can be fed without breaking the piggy bank. It's worth noting that Pistol Pete's does *not* bother trying to convince anybody it has the best pizza. If you see the chain's commercials and are taking a date to a movie, Pistol Pete's is *not* the place you'll stop at afterward. This chain has locked its sights on a very specific, identifiable, identified starving crowd. Those the chain's after know it's for them.

In Las Vegas, for many years, most casino-hotels aggressively pursued the business of the "high rollers." An acquaintance of mine has the title "Casino Host" at one of the biggest hotels on the Strip; he's actually a recruiter, who goes to other hotels, to parties in Beverly Hills and New York where the rich gather, even to Japan, to invite and inveigle high rollers to come to the hotel he represents—then, when they do, they are his honored and privileged guests, with complimentary rooms, meals, shows, airfare, limousines, even escorts if desired. Every big casino operation has such people. One high roller I know described Las Vegas as "the home of the $10,000 free drink."

Bob Stupak, mentioned earlier, ignored this market almost entirely. Nothing he did was targeted at the high roller. To the contrary, his market was middle income, middle America, mom 'n' pop, everyday folks, many of them first-time visitors to Glitter City. While the others chased the Saks customer, Bob preferred Sears. If the other hotels get people with Cadillacs, Mercedes, and even Rolls-Royces in their garages, Bob attracted the people with three-year-old station wagons. While the other hotels pursued the country-club crowd, Bob recruited at the bowling alleys. Today, the entire Las Vegas casino industry has refocused its sights on families, with such remarkable success that Las Vegas has surpassed even Florida as the number one family vacation destination in the United States.

These business leaders have very carefully tailored and very systematically delivered the right message to the right target markets. Different targets chosen, but success achieved because of targeting. A great deal can be gained by emulating their examples.

4

PROVING YOUR CASE

Like it or not, I don't believe one damned thing you tell me.

If we made a list of just the *big scandals* since Watergate, we'd fill a book. Richard Nixon taught us that we cannot trust our president. As a result, he dramatically altered the way in which the media treats political leaders and investigates and reports political shenanigans. Most media experts agree that John Kennedy would never get away with his now known but once secret sexual liaisons in today's climate. Clinton proved that to be true. Today, the public looks at every politician with a jaundiced eye.

Jim Bakker went to prison, Jimmy Swaggart became a shadow of his former self, and the entire evangelism field was damaged and shrunken thanks to the revealed financial misconduct and sexual philandering. A young woman came forward with revelations of long-term affairs with a succession of Catholic priests, the last winding up as the father of her child. These and many similar incidents have taught us we cannot trust our clergy.

All over the country, onetime pillars of their communities were tarred in the savings-and-loan disaster. In Miami, the CenTrust Tower became a monument to monumental fraud. In my home city of Phoenix, the Phoenician Resort built by Charlie Keating serves as a nagging, flamboyant reminder of excess. This enormously expensive scandal taught us that we cannot trust our bankers.

Chrysler Corporation got caught playing a game usually restricted to small-time tote-the-note car dealers: rolling back the odometer. Exxon dumped a boatload of oil on the Alaska coast, promised to clean it up, and then took a hike. Recently, major-name insurance corporations' and hospitals' executives have been prosecuted for massive financial fraud. These and countless other similarly shocking big-business misdeeds have clearly taught Americans that they cannot trust the Fortune 500.

The American public has been lied to so much by so many that we no longer trust anybody. In fact, research I've been privy to, thanks to the Guthy-Renker Corporation's expensive consumer focus groups, shows that they passionately distrust as a first instinct. Make no mistake about it: this is the Age of Skepticism.

There is an old joke—told to me by a very cynical businessman—about the father who puts his three-year-old son up on the fireplace mantle and holds out his hands and urges him to jump. "I'll catch you," he promises. After much coaxing and coercion, the kid jumps toward Daddy, who steps back and lets him crash to the floor. He then leans over the wailing youngster and says: "You've just learned your first great lesson of life—don't trust anybody."

The consumer and the business customer, your prospective customer or client, has been coerced off the mantle and let crash to the floor one too many times. Lucy has pulled the football away at the last minute one time too many, and Charlie Brown won't play anymore.

ULTIMATE MARKETING SECRET WEAPON #6
MARKETING MESSAGES DEVELOPED WITH THE UNDERSTANDING THAT RECIPIENTS WILL BE STUBBORNLY RELUCTANT TO BELIEVE THEM

A client came to me recently with a most interesting marketing problem: a truly irresistible offer that didn't work. His product is a certificate good for at least $500 worth of travel, including two nights in any one of several dozen good hotels scattered around the country, a $400 discount. You can take a three-day cruise for just $99 per person, and more. He sells these certificates to various businesses to use as premiums and incentives, at only 5¢—that's right!—5¢ each! The ultimate recipient of the certificate needs only to pay a $10 processing fee to use it, and my client has made that ridiculously easy: call a 900 number, hear a message about a trip and tour offers, and a $10 charge appears on your telephone bill.

Unfortunately, he's been having a tough time getting businesses to buy and use these things. And he's finding that a shockingly small percentage of the people who get them make the call to redeem them. How can this be? "Why," he asked, "doesn't this work better than it does?"

By now, of course, the answer is obvious, isn't it? The darned offer is just too good to be true. People don't believe it.

Today, if you make any kind of a free or big-discount offer, the consumer says to himself or herself: "Who's he kidding? Nothing's free. There's got to be a catch here somewhere." Or: "50 percent off, my eye! All they've done is jacked up the price so they can mark it back down. It's all baloney."

My research indicates that people don't even believe guarantees. They say: "Yeah, just try to get your money back. You've got to bring it back still wrapped in the original plastic, fill out a sixteen-part form, stand in line for three hours, and scream and yell and threaten their lives."

If you use testimonials—and I'm going to tell you that you should—they say: "I'll bet those are actors" or "I'll bet they're just made up" or "I'll bet they paid those people to say those things."

SO, HOW DO WE PROVE OUR CASE?

I sat, as an uninvolved observer, in the giant, lavishly decorated law firm conference room and watched and listened as one of this country's most famous trial attorneys conducted his pretrial conference with his associates, investigators, researchers, and paralegals. Each person summarized his or her work and each gave an opinion on the probable outcome.

One young attorney assured the boss, "I think you've got enough evidence to win this thing."

The boss came unglued. He slammed his hands down on the table and rocked the room. He lunged across the table, grabbed the young guy by his Brooks Brothers lapels, yanked him up, faced him nose-tip to nose-tip and bellowed loud enough to be heard on the opposite coast: "*Do not ever send me into a courtroom to face a jury with just enough evidence.*" He paused, dropped the shocked attorney back into his chair, walked to the end of the room and wrote these words on the blackboard:

PREPONDERANCE OF PROOF

Webster defines preponderance as a superiority in weight, power, importance, strength, or quantity. Roget's Thesaurus suggests these synonyms: majority, plurality, advantage, supremacy, maximum, lion's share, excess, surplus, redundancy, and domination. I suggest that you want all that and more when you present your case to the customer.

HOW TO GO FROM ZERO TO MAXIMUM CREDIBILITY

If we wanted an example of an industry with near-zero credibility, we need look no further than the people and businesses behind the automobile sitting outside in the driveway. Automobile salespeople are distrusted by everybody.

My own informal—but I think fairly accurate—survey shows that, ranked at the very bottom of the credibility ladder by the public are medical doctors, then lawyers, then, still worse, politicians, then, worst of all, car salesmen. And, quite frankly, in my opinion, they deserve this. If any other industry played the pricing games that the car dealers get away with, everybody would be in jail. Typically, people in the automobile business use artificial retail prices in order to create phony discounts, they advertise stripped models in order to play bait-and-switch, they use deceptive sales practices, they bully their customers, they sell grossly overpriced insurance add-ons, and they are notorious for lousy service after the sale. Both the Federal Trade Commission and the Attorney Generals of this country should be ashamed of themselves for permitting this stuff to continue.

However, there are good, honest, reputable exceptions to this rule.

The most honest and, I think, not coincidentally, the most successful automobile salesman I know is Bill Glazner at Sanderson Ford here in Phoenix. He has managed to attain maximum credibility in a business that, overall, has no credibility—a tough task, but a great marketing lesson.

When you go to buy a car from Bill, like most anywhere else, you go out on the lot and look at cars, kick tires, maybe test drive a couple. Eventually you are led down the hall where the long row of salesmen's cubicles are placed. These are pretty much the same everywhere. You've been in more than one. The walls are ticky-tacky plywood partitions held in place with the little screw-doo-dads we had on pole lamps in the sixties. In each cubicle, there's a basic military-issue gray or green metal desk. There are two turquoise or orange plastic stackable chairs for the customers. And that is it.

Bill's cubicle is the same as the others you've seen—except for one little detail. Floor to ceiling, side to side, every square inch of wall space is covered with instant snapshots of Bill's customers, proudly posed next to their new cars, with their names and dates of purchase written on them. I have never counted the photos, but the quantity is overwhelming. Then, look a little closer and you'll pick up two patterns in the arrangement of the snapshots. First, the relationship pattern. For example, next to the picture of me with my Lincoln, you'll see the photo of my wife with her Taurus, my parents with their Mercury, my brother with his pickup truck, my business partner with his Lincoln, his wife with her Probe, his sales manager with his Tempo, and one of his office managers with his Escort. Also, you'll see a historical pattern. Not just me with my current Lincoln, but backwards chronologically to me with the Lincoln before that. In some cases, there will be five, even six such photos: the customer with his new car, the same customer with the car he bought in 1997, again with the car he bought in 1994, again with the car he bought in 1991.

Now I'm going to tell you something that is almost unbelievable. I've gone there with my wife, with business associates, and with friends while they bought cars from Bill and I have watched, in every case, as Bill figured up the price, wrote it on the contract, and quoted the price and payment amounts, and heard the customers say, "Fine." I've watched them sign on the dotted line without even once haggling over price. In the car business!

In the weight-loss business, one very successful sales representative for diet products carries a sales tool with her everywhere she goes: a photo blown up into a life-size poster of herself, fifty-four pounds heavier than she is today. She unrolls the poster and stands next to it, and the sale is made.

Some 25 years ago, I was at an Amway Rally where the guest speakers were Charlie and Elsie Marsh, enormously successful distributors. The experience stuck in my mind so that I'm still using it as an example today. You need to understand that Amway uses a multilevel marketing system, where distributors recruit others who recruit others, etc., and earn overrides on the performance of everybody "down line" from them and those they recruit. Distributors need to be convinced that the plan really works and that they can, in fact, build a large organization and income by recruiting.

Charlie pulled a half-dozen volunteers out of the audience up onto the auditorium's stage, and they started at one end of the stage and unfolded a huge, five-foot-high and 50-foot-wide hunk of posterboard with Charlie's immense distributor organization diagrammed out, with each distributor's name and home city listed next to the little circle that represented them. The thousands and thousands of connected circles all emanated from about 15 people Charlie had personally recruited into the business. He said, "If you know 15 people, you can do this, too."

When you walk into my chiropractor's office, you'll see one wall almost entirely covered with instant snapshots of the practitioner standing next to each smiling, happy patient. You see, these pictures are *instantly convincing*.

ULTIMATE MARKETING SECRET WEAPON #7
PICTURES THAT PROVE YOUR CASE

Let me tell you something funny. Bill Glazner's been outperforming his sales colleagues at Sanderson Ford month after month, year after year—yet he's the only salesman there with photographs up on his cubicle walls. In the diet products company the lady with the life-size "before" poster sells for, there are over 15,000 representatives, but as far as I know only one has a poster of her overweight former self.

The night I saw Charlie Marsh unroll his organizational chart, there were at least *500* Amway distributors in the audience, many of whom I knew then and know today. To the best of my knowledge, nobody "stole" Charlie's idea.

From 1983 to 1987, I built the largest integrated seminar and publishing firm exclusively teaching marketing to chiropractors and dentists, and, in one way or another, I told all of these stories to at least 15,000 doctors during those years. Since then, I've addressed a number of large audiences in these professions and I'm a contributing editor to *The Successful Practice Newsletter*—and I'm still telling these same stories to the doctors. Yet, to the best of my knowledge, there's only one with a photo wall.

Maybe all that is a comment on my effectiveness. I hope not. I think not. Instead, I think it is simply a reflection of the vast majority's interest in improving, but only if doing so requires no change, discomfort, or initiative. That's why, in every field, a few out-earn the huge "mediocre majority" by giant margins.

WHO SAYS SO?

What others say about you, your company, your products, and your services is infinitely more credible than anything you can say on your own behalf. When you make a statement, it's a claim. When your satisfied customer makes the same statement about you, that's a *fact*.

I am here to tell you that you cannot overuse testimonials.

Some businesses, notably the weight-loss industry, do an outstanding job of getting and using good testimonials—watch advertising by Weight Watchers or Richard Simmons' TV infomercials. During the time I was writing the first edition of this book, Citibank was running a very effective series of TV commercials for their VISA card, featuring real people telling of the help they got from Citibank when they lost their cards or when they needed additional credit. Another testimonial-driven TV campaign of a very similar nature had Lee Iaccoca personally interviewing car accident victims saved by Chrysler's air bags. What these people said was believable. It had the obvious ring of truth. In Citibank's case, it made the incredible credible, the unbelievable believable; that a bank really cares about its customers and will quickly respond to their special needs and problems, any time, 24 hours a day.

This strategy will never go out of style, never run out of gas. Right now, as I'm writing the new edition of this book, late in 1999, the "sweepstakes industry," including Publishers Clearinghouse and American Family Publishers, is reeling from regulatory agency attacks and huge quantities of negative media coverage. Their response has been to step up their testimonial-driven advertising, showing off their happy winners more than ever. Priceline.com, a new business that's the name-your-price marketer of travel on the Internet, tries to convince the public to use a new and different way of buying airline tickets by running full-page magazine ads filled with photographs of happy Priceline customers captioned with the trips they took and the amounts of money they saved.

But now I'm going to let you in on a "secret." As common and well-proven as testimonial use is, the absence or underuse of testimonials remains *the* number one marketing error I see repeated most frequently. For example, in many of my audio cassette courses (and in this book's companion, *The Ultimate Sales Letter*), I give out "Critique Coupons" that entitle people to send in their ads, brochures, sales letters, or other marketing materials for my critique. Some months I handle hundreds of these. I'd guess that I responded to at least a few thousand last year alone.

They come from every imaginable kind of business; from the butchers, bakers, and candlestick makers of the world; from marketing novices but also from people who ought to know the basics. Without question, the suggestion I send back to these folks so frequently I get sick of saying it is:

"Hey, where are your testimonials?"

I can promise you this: if you get nothing else out of this entire book but the inspiration to collect and heavily use as many good testimonials as you can possibly get, you'll have a strong competitive advantage from that alone.

WHAT IS A GOOD TESTIMONIAL?

For starters, think of a testimonial as a pair of verbal "snapshots." The first is the "Before" picture—the problem or the skepticism; the second is the "After" picture—the positive result, the pleasant surprise, the solution. "I was fat, lonely, frightened, poor, unhappy, skeptical, etc.—now, thanks to XYZ, I'm thin, popular, confident, rich, happy, and a believer!"

Second, view testimonials as strategic weapons. I suggest making two lists: one of every claim, feature, benefit, and fact about what you're marketing that you want to substantiate; second, every doubt, fear, or question that might exist in your prospective customer's mind. Then collect and use testimonials that specifically substantiate the claims and eliminate the doubts.

A FEW EXAMPLES

A cafeteria wants to attract new customers. The owners are eager to emphasize the variety of foods they offer and that, unlike some cafeterias, they keep their food hot and fresh. The owners also know there are a great many people who never dream of coming to a cafeteria. Against that, they position these testimonials:

> I haven't eaten in a cafeteria since high school, but I'm sure glad a friend brought me here—I'm really surprised at the tremendous variety that's offered. Finally there's someplace I can take the whole family for dinner and make everybody happy.

> I've always thought that cafeteria food sat around on hot plates and got soggy. Maybe that is true elsewhere, but everything here is piping hot, fresh, and, well, really good.

A dentist "made hay" with this great testimonial:

> I avoided dental care I knew I needed for almost a year because I didn't want the pain. I just couldn't stand the thought of going to the dentist. But I've got to say that Dr. Welmer and his staff were just terrific! They were patient and understanding. And things sure have changed since the last time I went to a dentist. Dr. Welmer's got the newest technology so the treatment was virtually pain-free. I was amazed.

And this powerful testimonial for a lawn service:

> I'm busy, I travel a lot on business, and I hate taking care of my lawn. It always needed to be cut. Plants died. I tried different lawn care guys—you know, the guys with beat-up old pickup trucks who come around and hang Xeroxed flyers on your door, then never show up when they're supposed to. When the representative of Lawn Technicians knocked on my door and I agreed to use them, I was prepared for another aggravating disappointment. Now, three months later, I'm telling everybody I know to use Lawn Technicians. They've turned lawn care into a profession.

THE EXPANDED TESTIMONIAL

In print advertising, you'll usually see short testimonials, two or three sentences long. On TV and radio, they're usually a few seconds, except in 30-minute long infomercials, where each testimonial may run for a couple of minutes. Even though short is the norm, there may be cases where you'll want to use an expanded testimonial. I've seen entire ads built around a single testimonial, like the ones shown on the following pages.

Another use of the expanded testimonial is in article form. Some magazines, especially trade magazines, have an unwritten policy of giving advertisers editorial space without added cost along with the ad space. This is common in the business opportunity field, with magazines like *Spare Time* and *Moneymaking Opportunities*. Reprinted on page 60 is an "article" I wrote for a client, U.S. Gold Chain, and furnished to the magazine. To the reader, it seems like an article. For the client/advertiser, it's really an extended testimonial.

Family Discovers Amazing Part Time Profits

Carolyn and Bob Harniss of Barberton, Ohio had good jobs — he managed an office supply warehouse store and she was a receptionist at an insurance company. After four years of marriage, they were living well but not extravagantly, saving some money but still a long way away from having the money needed for a down payment on a new home.

One day, Carolyn found an ad of U.S. Gold Chain in *Money Making Opportunities Magazine*. This company's "Gold By The Inch" business opportunity sounded good to her so she tore out the ad and showed it to her husband. She says, "I told Bob that everyone loves gold jewelry. I think it would be easy to sell this gold in lots of different ways. Maybe we could make enough money with this business to buy a new home."

Although Bob was a little skeptical about the whole idea, they sent for the catalog and then, after looking it over, sent for the $399.00 Starter Kit. "Frankly, I went along at Carolyn's insistence," Bob admits. "I figured if worst came to worst, we could sell enough of the chains to friends and people we knew to get our money back and then give the rest away as gifts."

When the Starter Kit arrived a few days later, Bob changed his mind. "I was surprised to find everything needed to operate this as a real business. There was even a video tape that showed us exactly how to make the chain and how easy it is to sell it." In the Starter Kit, U.S. Gold Chain provides 12 spools of the most popular styles of beautiful gold-layered chains, the clasps and tools to create the jewelry on the spot, a large, attention-getting sign plus Manufacturers Lifetime Guarantee Certificates for the customers! The kit, which costs only $399.00, has enough inventory in it to produce over $3,000 in profits for the Distributor.

On the first weekend after receiving the Starter Kit, Carolyn and Bob went out to a swap meet in their area. Carolyn recalls, "We were just amazed at the interest that people had in Gold By The Inch. There was a crowd of people around our booth from mid-morning to the end of the day."

"My fingers were actually a little sore from making the chains," Bob says, "but I didn't care. We sold over $450 worth of chains that weekend. Because of the huge markup on Gold By The Inch, that represented about $400 in clear profits for us. About $200 a day! We had recovered our entire investment and still had a large inventory of chains to sell."

Bob and Carolyn had dinner on Sunday with her parents and her father commented that he had never heard of a business you could start that easily and recover your start-up costs so quickly. He then called a friend who owned a greeting card store in a local shopping mall and arranged a meeting between Carolyn and Bob with this man. That led to them putting a Gold By The Inch set-up in the front of that store and the following weekend, they sold nearly $1,000 worth of chains. When Carolyn's father saw how well they did, he had to get involved. Now they have two and sometimes three locations operating almost every weekend. Carolyn explains, "Bob, I, my Dad and sometimes my younger brother work the locations and share the profits."

"We've been Gold By The Inch distributors for almost a year and we've put over $11,000 into the savings account for the down-payment on our house. We're going to buy our new home early next year," says Bob. In the meantime, Carolyn has quit her job and is devoting her time to managing and expanding the business. Both Carolyn and Bob agree that this has been the best move they have ever made!

Gold By The Inch distributors did over $20,000,000 worth of business last year and they have only scratched the surface of the demand for gold chains. There is still a ground floor opportunity open with U.S. Gold Chain, a major force in the quality costume jewelry field.

You can receive a free information kit including a beautiful full color catalog and wholesale price list. Just write to U.S. Gold Chain Mfg. Co., Dept. MM-1, 11460 N. Cave Creek Rd., Phoenix, AZ 85020. If you would like a video tape that shows everything about the business, include a $10.00 refundable deposit when you write. Return the video within 30 days or place an order and your $10.00 will be refunded.

REAL PEOPLE VERSUS CELEBRITY TESTIMONIALS

Real People testimonials are, in my opinion, a mandatory component of a solid marketing message. These typically come from your satisfied customers. When using a number of these testimonials in one message, you want to try to cover as many claim-benefit bases and as many demographic bases as possible.

If marketing to a demographically diverse group of consumers, you need testimonials from whites, blacks, Asians, and Hispanics; men, women, married, and single people; and the old, the middle-aged, and the young.

If you're doing business-to-business marketing, the bases you might want to cover would include small companies, medium-sized companies, and big companies—as well as retailers, wholesalers, manufacturers, and service businesses. Of course, if you're aiming at a much more narrow, specific target market, then you can match your testimonial sources to it.

I consider it fair to coach and coax in order to get the testimonial comments you want, but unfair, and often also woefully ineffective, to put words in the mouths of people providing testimony.

Celebrity testimonials can be effective, but can also be tricky. If your product or service is used or your business patronized by a known personality, such as an athlete or entertainer, you can capitalize on it. Sometimes even an endorsement of your general industry is useful. Some years back, Roger Craig and Joe Montana, both then playing for the San Francisco 49ers football team, stated that they relied on chiropractors to keep them healthy. I said then, and I'll still say it today: any chiropractor not utilizing this is just plain dumb.

When marketing on a national scale, you need nationally known celebrities, but when marketing locally, a local personality is just about equal in impact but usually a lot easier and less costly to get. Two different chains of weight-loss clinics use the identical strategy of paying local radio disc jockeys and talk-show hosts to lose weight in their clinics, then serve as spokespersons in the commercials, giving personal testimony. This has proven extraordinarily effective for both companies.

In our market, I've seen a restaurant using the endorsement of a very popular former governor, car dealers using football players, a bank using a football coach, and a chiropractor using a woman rodeo star.

Keep in mind that there are different ways to be a celebrity. A person can be instantly recognizable because of his or her face, such as a famous TV personality. Or a person might go unrecognized in a crowd but still have celebrity value based on who they are and what they do. Ford Motor Company was able to use former auto racing champion Jackie Stewart very effectively, even though you'd probably bump into him on the street and not know him. Even people who are not instantly recognizable visually or by name can still lend celebrity value and credibility to a marketing message once it is explained who they are.

How many of these names are instantly recognizable to you: Joan Quigley, Walter Annenberg, Brendan Suhr, Robert Parker, Linda Bloodworth-Thomason? If you got even one of them, you're sharper than most. Still, by telling you who they are, I can use each of them effectively in certain marketing messages.

Joan Quigley was Nancy Reagan's astrologer. I worked on an infomercial featuring Joan promoting books and cassettes about astrology. Walter Annenberg was the publisher of *Parade Magazine*, which millions of families receive with their Sunday newspapers. Walter is a rags-to-riches Horatio Alger, discouraged from reading as a child, and now a dynamic spokesperson for literacy.

Walter could be very effectively used in marketing a book club membership, raising funds for public television, or, as I suggested one year, on an infomercial marketing an adult learn-to-read course. Brendan Suhr has been the assistant head coach of the Detroit Pistons and the Orlando Magic, and could be used in marketing sports equipment, athletic shoes, or even, as I've used him, in promoting a self-improvement course. Robert Parker is the author of the famous "Spenser" detective novels, on which the TV series that starred Robert Urich was based. Parker would be an excellent personality to build a solve-a-mystery cruise package around. Linda Bloodworth-Thomason is a very successful TV producer; her credits include producing the hit show *Designing Women*. Linda could be used in marketing some kind of how-to-break-into-show-business product or a career success product for women.

In the production of TV infomercials I've worked with Florence Henderson, famous as the mom of *The Brady Bunch*; Chris Robinson, probably best known for his eight-year stint as Dr. Eric Webber on the soap *General Hospital*; Gloria Loring, also a soap opera actress; Robb Weller, former host of *Entertainment Tonight*; and others. In marketing local projects, I've worked with local radio and television personalities in several cities. With only a few notable exceptions not named here, I've found both the celebrities and their agents to be pretty cooperative and pleasant to work with. Each of the ones I've named especially impressed me with his or her professionalism, ability, and sincere commitment to producing an effective project.

If you are seeking the services of a local celebrity, you can usually contact the person directly, or your advertising agency can track the person down for you and make a proposal to them. Many national celebrities can be found listed in the directories of the

Academy of Motion Picture Arts.* Or you can contact one of the big talent agencies, such as the William Morris Agency in Los Angeles.

THE IMPACT OF BULK

I have a friend and colleague in the speaking business who has no brochure, no demo cassette, no professional selling tools at all. When someone is interested in booking him, my friend sends a box—the kind and size that holds five hundred sheets of paper, like one you might buy at the office supply store—filled with copies of testimonial letters from his satisfied clients. I'm sure nobody sits and reads more than four hundred letters. They don't have to.

Reprinted at the end of this chapter is a "client list" from a catering company. It, too, is impressive due to quantity.

USE ALL THE FIRE POWER YOU CAN MUSTER

Today's smart marketer uses pictorial evidence, testimonials, client lists, satisfied customers, and celebrities—every ounce of social proof she can pull together—to prove her case.

---

*Academy of Motion Picture Arts Directory: Academy of Motion Pictures Arts & Sciences, 8949 Wilshire Boulevard, Beverly Hills, CA 90211, (213) 278-8990.

4522 N. 26th Drive • Phoenix, Arizona 85017 • (602) 242-2662

Catering For All Occasions
...Good Food...Good Service...

Weddings

Cookouts

Open Houses

Anniversaries

Church Functions

Office Parties

SHARKO'S CATERING has been serving the entire valley for over thirteen years. We look forward to be of service to you for any occasion.

We are proud to announce some of our previous clients:

Catered to POPE JOHN PAUL II ENTOURAGE while in Phoenix

Lou Grubb Car Dealership
Knoell Homes
Citibank
Century 21
The Hartford Insurance
Sears Stores
The Salvation Army
IBM
U.S.Express
Bradshaw & Viles
Serra Club
Kino Institute
Frazee Paint
United Pacific Insurance
Grunewald & Adams Fine Jewelers
Gannett Outdoor Co.
Skyway Management
MeraBank
Del E. Webb Corp.
U.S. West Directory
Arizona Lift Trucks
C.G. Rein Galleries
Sun Cities Art Museum
Nike
Heidelberg West

The Catholic Diocese of Phoenix
U.S. Navy Reserves
U.S. Marine Reserves
Society for Neuroscience
The Greyhound Corp.
Penneys Stores
Boys Club of Phoenis
Mardian Construction
Climate Control
MCI
Carson Messinger Elliot, etc.
(law firm)
Crampton Woods etc.(law firm)
O'Connor, Cavanaugh (law firm)
Air National Guard of Arizona
Simplex Time Recorder Co.
Blood Systems, Inc.
Desert X--Rays
Arizona Special Olympics
M/V Acceptance, Ltd.
Scottsdale Resort Apt. Hotel
Temple Solel
Cigna
The Arizona Republic/Phoenix
Gazette

SHARKO'S CLIENT LIST, P. 1

4522 N 26th Drive • Phoenix, Arizona 85017 • (602) 242-2662

Catering For All Occasions
...Good Food...Good Service...

Weddings

- 2 -

Cookouts	Levitz Furniture Corp.
	U.S. Recycling
	DMJM
	Eason & Waller
	Phoenix Heat Treating Corp.
	Phoenix Distr. Co.
	Phillips & Lyon (law firm)
Open Houses	Amica Insurance
	Transamerica Insurance
	Systems Marketing, Inc.
	Neutron Industries
	Realty Executives
	Continental Insurance
	Casa Santa Cruz
Anniversaries	American Resort Residential
	Developers, Inc.
	Dun &Bradstreet
	Dial One
	Telemation
	Goldwater Stores
Church Functions	Murray Peck, P.C.
	Fremont Indemnity Co.
	Mazak
	Hill Bros. Chemical Co.
	Linda Brock car dealership
	Lynndale Stainless Service, Inc.
Office Parties	Rivera & Scales, P.C.
	Lyon Commercial Brokerage Co.
	Nevada Federal Credit Union
	National Brands, Inc.

Sun Insurance Agency
The Sun Eagle Corp.
P A C of Arizona
Powerwall Corp.
Presto Casting Co.
Phoenix & Valley of the Sun
   Convention & Visitors Bureau
Prestige Cleaners
Realty World
Eastman Kodak Co.
Scientific-Atlanta
Sun City Water Co.
P.I.P.E.
Swiss-America Trading Corp.
Western International University
Turf Paradise, Inc.
Select Drywall
Shannon & Cronin (law firm)
Valley National Bank
Tech Plastics Inc.
Turner Ranches
Valley Neurology Associates, Ltd.
Harris Data Service
Wisniewski Surrano (law firm)
Westernaires
The Tanner Companies
Westbrook Village
DeMuro Enterprises, Inc.
American Home Shield
Louis P. Ferrara (law firm)
+ many, many more!

SHARKO'S CLIENT LIST, P. 2

5

PUTTING
YOUR BEST FOOT
FORWARD

I have, on many occasions, been paid as a consultant to visit a chiropractor's office, tour it, check out the office's new-patient procedures, and evaluate what might be done better in order to make patients comfortable, confident, satisfied, and likely to refer. Frankly, an amazing number of times, my best advice has had to do with some 75-watt light bulbs and a bottle of Mr. Clean. Which brings us to a discussion of image, specifically "business image."

Let's begin inside your business, at its premises. This is relevant to the degree that your customers, vendors, investors, or community members visit your business location. If no one ever visits, there's nominal damage done by a pigsty location. If even one person visits, the damage begins.

The Minit-Lube example is instructive; these guys stole an entire business right out from under the service-station owners and operators, virtually overnight, with a remarkably simple strategy: a pleasant environment. Perhaps you've taken your car to a service station and waited while getting an oil change. The waiting area had old, peeling linoleum covered with grease and two plastic chairs to sit on; a stack of hot-rod magazines; a coffee maker surrounded by styrofoam cups and utensils. Now with that memory clearly fixed in your mind, go visit a Minit-Lube (or any of its regional kindred, such as Jiffy Lube). I don't need to describe the difference. Or the difference it has made in where America gets its oil changed.

Another industry that has undergone a similar metamorphosis is the instant, or storefront, printing business, led in its image conversion by an Arizona-based franchiser of Alpha-Graphics.

These innovators have applied lessons learned from Walt Disney and Ray Kroc: even simple cleanliness can be a powerful marketing tool.

Here's a very simple, two-question test to apply to your own business premises and everything that is seen, heard, touched, smelled, tasted, or experienced there:

Question #1
In ten words or less, describe the image you want your business to project.

Question #2
Does everything contribute to projecting that image?

Let me give you a great example of incongruity. For several years, I owned and drove a Cadillac; in recent years I've chosen Lincolns. When I had my Caddy, I had it serviced at the best, most successful, most respected Cadillac dealership in Phoenix. As you might guess, their new-car showroom was immaculate: windows sparkling clean, floor buffed to a high gloss, lighting just so, unobtrusive music playing softly in the background.

Their service department was also smartly run. During morning rush hour, when many people dropped off their cars, neatly dressed young women greeted the customers and offered them coffee. The service technicians were also nicely dressed, with shirts and neckties. The area was kept pretty much free of grease and grime. There was also an air of efficiency that was reassuring. The service technicians each had computer terminals and could pull up your car's service records. From the screen, they knew and didn't have to ask for your name, address, phone number, etc.

So far, so good.

The first incongruity was, I suppose, relatively minor, yet it certainly made a major, lasting impression on my mind: the courtesy cars they used to drop customers off at their offices were Buicks, not Cadillacs.

The second incongruity looms larger: the place where you settled your account was sandwiched into a narrow hallway; you stood not in a line, for which there was no room, but rather in an intimate, pushing, annoying cluster of people; you conversed with the clerks through tiny little windows; and the clerk I dealt with on two occasions chewed and popped bubble-gum and was devoid of personality.

What's wrong with that picture? A lot. To be consistent with the image being conveyed by all other areas of the operation, there should have been a nicely appointed, living-room type of area where the customers sat comfortably and the clerks came to them, got the invoices signed, took the credit cards back to the accounting area, processed them there, and brought the finished paperwork back to the customer with a smile and a thank you.

ULTIMATE MARKETING SECRET WEAPON #8
IMAGE CONGRUENCY

Every piece of your "puzzle" should be strategically crafted to reinforce a single, central image.

I'd suggest, incidentally, that "successful" be part of the image you choose to convey. I find that, in most businesses, customers prefer dealing with successful businesses and businesspeople.

I can recall going with a consulting client of mine when he was interviewing and choosing a new attorney for his firm—his company was in considerable difficulty with the Federal Trade Commission at the time so he was going to be a fat catch for whichever law firm he selected. I thought the conversation with the two lawyers at the first firm went well, but he was skeptical about them when we left. He admitted that he couldn't put his finger on why he was uncomfortable with them; he just was. It was several hours later that the impression maneuvered from his subconscious to his conscious and he was able to enunciate his reason for discomfort: "Nothing," he said, "was going on." The phones weren't ringing; the receptionist was reading a magazine; there were empty word-processor work areas; there was no typing noise. In his mind he translated that, rightly or wrongly—but in marketing, perception *is* reality—to the law firm being unsuccessful.

Once I was counseling a chiropractor, brand new in practice, located in a brand new shopping center at a busy intersection but too new to be fully occupied with tenants. He was suffering from an inordinately high number of "no shows": people who would respond to his advertising, schedule exam appointments, then not show up.

His parking lot was nude.

He and his staff parked their own cars behind the center. His practice was so new there were rarely patients' cars parked there. And there were no adjacent tenants creating traffic. "How would you feel," I asked him, "if you started to drive up here for your first appointment?" We got his car, his staff's cars, and a couple of rented-by-the-week Cadillacs parked in front of that office; his no-show rate dropped like a rock.

CREATING A MARKETING-ORIENTED STORE ENVIRONMENT

If you don't have a store, you're welcome to skip this brief section.

Coincidentally and fortunately, I was at a major shopping mall recently, and, in a national chain store I won't name here, overheard one well-dressed woman, I'd guess rather affluent, say to her shopping companion, "Let's go—this place is too confusing. I can't find what I want here."

I can't count how many times I've seen a store environment or at least part of a store environment designed for the convenience of the staff—not the customer! The smart store environment quite simply facilitates buying. That should be the primary consideration in every design and display decision: does it make it easier and more likely that the customer will buy?

Last week, I was in a men's clothing store and was struck by these oddities:

1. The casual slacks, like jeans and twill slacks, were intermingled with the dress slacks.
2. The necktie display was closer to the sport shirts than to the dress shirts.
3. Shoes were displayed only in the window, then all the way at the rear of the store.
4. The walls in the dressing rooms were blank.

What would you do differently?

I think I'd group my sports clothes together in one area, and display casual slacks, shirts, jackets, and shoes there. I'd similarly group my dress slacks, dress shirts, ties, jackets, suits, and dress shoes together. I'd put framed photos of my newest fashions up on the walls of the dressing rooms.

Here's my Five-Point Criteria for smart store design:

1. Conveys a congruent, deliberate image.
2. Presents goods in a logical, organized way.
3. Helps the customer think with "creative idea displays."

(I was in a pet store recently and—lo and behold—in the fish section, they had a display featuring everything you'd need to set up your first tropical fish aquarium: the aquarium itself, the underground filter, a bag of gravel, a stand, a light and hood, and so on, each neatly labeled with what it was and what it did. Over by the cute puppies was a similar display titled "The Family's First Dog," and it displayed a bowl, bag of food, box of vitamins, a couple of chew toys, a brush, a collar, a leash, and so on.)

4. Educates the customer when appropriate—by display, by continuous-loop video, by live demonstrator.
5. Utilizes every possibility—such as wall space—to promote, advertise, and educate.

Some store environment principles apply to nonstore locations, too, even including professional offices. I teach chiropractors, for example, that there are only three reasons for the patient being in the office:

1. to get well
2. to learn how to stay well
3. to get inspired to refer

and that every minute spent there, and everything seen or heard while there should be related to one, two, or all three of those reasons. That means: out with the magazines, in with interesting, educational literature; out with the background music, in with continuous-loop video; out with the mass-produced paintings of farmhouses and snowcapped mountains, in with charts and posters.

An accountant accidentally heard me talking to a group of chiropractors about this and cornered me after the seminar. "How can I apply that idea to my office?" he wanted to know. I asked him, "What are your clients there for? What services do you offer that most clients need but few use?"

We agreed that his clients were there, first, to get well organized financially; second, to learn how to work in tandem with him to stay that way; and third, to get inspired to refer. We determined that financial planning and estate planning were little-used services. So, out with the magazines, in with interesting, education literature; out with the background music, in with a continuous- loop video about financial planning and estate planning; out with the F. W. Woolworth paintings, in with relevant posters and signs. And, without a nickel of external advertising, his practice increased its total services rendered to existing clients by more than 30 percent and doubled its client base through referrals in a year.

I think just about any business can turn its environment into a much more effective marketing-oriented environment with these ideas.

CONSIDER YOUR COMMUNITY IMAGE, TOO

Smart businesses make a point of being visibly good corporate citizens. That starts with being careful not to have policies or procedures with a high risk of offending a significant segment of your community.

Consider the famous story about Stew Leonard's well-known supermarket, where one customer went through the checkout line with several bags of groceries only to discover she had left wallet, checkbook, credit cards, and identification at home. The cashier or cashier-area manager made the decision to "gamble" a hundred bucks or so worth of groceries on the eternal goodwill of that customer and her circle of influence and let her take the food home and bring the money back the next day.

You have to consider the impact of your policies and procedures on the image you are working to sustain and convey.

An excellent community image strategy is allying your business with one or two noncontroversial, nonpolitical, highly respected nonprofit organizations or charitable causes. You don't necessarily have to be a big business to get big recognition from this sort of thing.

There's a very small chain of three stores here in Phoenix that, year after year, with money raised from company employees and customers—not from corporate coffers—is a very prominent, visible sponsor of the Arthritis Foundation's annual telethon. This little company gets tens of thousands of dollars' worth of free advertising on radio and television. By becoming active as a supporter of this type of organization, you also meet and get to network with other influential, progressive people in your community.

BOOSTING YOUR IMAGE WITH A CELEBRITY SPOKESPERSON

The best known commercial spokesperson of all time is, ironically, a fictional character: Betty Crocker. For over 75 years, Betty Crocker has been a symbol of helpfulness, a spokesperson for quality. She began in 1921 just as a signature for responses to letters from buyers of Gold Medal Flour. In 1924, she was given a voice for daytime radio and, over time, over one million women enrolled in "The Betty Crocker Cooking School of the Air." In 1950, the fictional Betty became the bestselling author of *The Betty Crocker Cookbook*. And this make-believe personality continues to serve its company well today.

A client of mine, Florida Communities/Intercoastal Communities, a major developer of retirement communities, benefited tremendously from having George Gobel, Ol' Lonesome George, as their spokesperson, and they used him extensively: on video, on audio tapes, in their literature, as a signer of letters, in cardboard cut-out form to greet newcomers to their communities, even with his voice answering their phones, until he passed away.

These two examples demonstrate that you don't need to have a "giant celebrity" in order to benefit from celebrity endorsement.

In fact, on a national level, on TV commercials, in TV infomercials, and in print, you are often better served by a much less costly *Love Boat* celebrity—meaning someone who would be guest-starring on *Love Boat* or *Murder She Wrote* every so often, if those shows were still on. Entertainment personalities not necessarily in the prime of their careers but still very well known to your target market. Right now, we aging baby-boomers are more familiar with the stars of re-runs than current TV.

You don't have to be a big company, though, to connect with a celebrity spokesperson. Working in the infomercial industry for the last 15 years, I've had the privilege of working on projects with Florence Henderson; soap stars Gloria Loring and Chris Robinson; game-show host Bob Eubanks; former *Entertainment Tonight* host Robb Weller; NFL great Fran Tarkenton; and dozens of other celebrities. I've had the experience of dealing with their agents, business managers, and attorneys. And I am here to tell you that linking your business to a celebrity spokesperson can cost a lot less than you would guess. A nationally recognized celebrity perfectly matched to your type of product, service, or business can be brought to your team for as little as $15,000 to, more commonly, $25,000 to $50,000 per year. If you divide that by the number of transactions or customers in a year, or even by calendar days, it's a pittance, and it has to produce a very small bump in most businesses' sales to justify itself.

A local celebrity can cost even less, and, for many local businesses, that local celeb is just as valuable as a big-name Hollywood star.

Here in Phoenix, we have an RV dealership using a recently retired, very popular local sportscaster in its TV commercials very effectively and, I'm sure, without breaking its budget.

BOOSTING YOUR IMAGE WITH BRAND-NAME IDENTITY

For years, when you went to the grocery store or supermarket to buy some chicken for the Saturday afternoon backyard barbecue, you bought chicken, period. Just chicken, on a cardboard tray, wrapped with plastic wrap by the grocer. But Frank Perdue used himself as a spokesperson and his name to proprietize chicken, and today people go to the store looking for Perdue Chicken. Of course, there's also Jimmy Dean Sausage and Bob Evans Farm Sausage.

If you look in your Yellow Pages under "Plumbing," you'll probably find a big ad featuring George Brazil Plumbing, with a choice of phone numbers for different areas in your locale. And if you call, the plumber who comes to your home will be in a clean, neatly pressed uniform with the George Brazil logo.

Actually, this is nothing more than a national advertising identity, a form of a brand name, which individual plumbers in each area pay for the right to use. This gives each plumber a big image boost over other independent operators.

In many respects, the George Brazil character is to plumbing what Betty Crocker is to baked goods. In other ways, you might compare George Brazil to Century 21 in real estate—not really a national chain, actually a brand name.

HOW DO YOU DECIDE WHAT MOVIE TO SEE?

I've always found the movie I wanted to see and then gone to whatever theater it was playing at that was closest to my house, and I'm sure others use that same process. But a recent "Best of Phoenix" survey showed me that a lot of moviegoers use a very different process: they prefer and deliberately choose to go to Harkins Theaters. We have here in our area theaters owned by several national chains, like General Theaters. Harkins happens to be a small, locally owned chain, and its brand name is recognized by many theatergoers as number one in quality and value. This chain has the cleanest theaters, most comfortable seats, and best gourmet snacks, and many people look in the newspaper *first* for Harkins' ads, then choose among the movies playing at Harkins, rather than choosing a movie first and then deciding on the theater. It proves that even a small, local business can create strong brand name identity in the marketplace and profit tremendously as a result.

GETTING FREE ADVERTISING

PUBLICITY AND PUBLIC RELATIONS

I'll bet you've heard the old adage, "There's no such thing as bad press." It is often quoted. It's also ridiculous. Ask Exxon. Ask some of the companies that have been destroyed, and I do mean destroyed, some justly but some unjustly, by TV's pseudonews programs like *2020* or *60 Minutes*. Yes, you can tell it's going to be a bad day when Mike Wallace is waiting for you when you arrive at the office.

The first rule of getting good publicity is to avoid bad publicity.

Some years back, in an incredibly stupid move, AmericaWest airlines published an article in its company newsletter by one of its preferred-provider doctors in which he called chiropractic "a cult" and compared chiropractic treatment to "a shampoo and a set." The M.D. who wrote this article must have been on another planet when the chiropractic profession won its lawsuit against the AMA, prompted by just such remarks as his. But it is inconceivable that a generally savvily run, large corporation would permit material certain to be offensive to a large constituency to appear in print under its name.

The backlash was fast and big. *The Chiropractic Journal,* a newspaper with a reach that includes about 10,000 chiropractors in AmericaWest's prime market areas of Arizona, Nevada, and California, devoted not just column inches but pages to savaging the airline. Hundreds of chiropractors called and cancelled flight reservations. Practice-management firms holding meetings urged attending practitioners to fly other airlines. Many Phoenix chiropractors distributed literature to all their patients criticizing the airline.

I can't speculate about what the airline lost as a result of all this. It could have been worse; the airline was fortunate the local news media didn't make a story out of it. But I can tell you they won nothing and lost something. The person at the helm of a business has to carefully scrutinize every advertisement, press release, publication, verbal statement, product name—everything—and ask: is there any way this can blow up in my face?

In the entertainment business, there's a country-and-western singer who did immeasurable damage to her career by attacking the beef industry. She may have thought the media attention of the moment was pretty nifty, but over the long haul she's found sponsors for concerts and TV shows, guest invitations to talk shows, and other important advantages hard to come by. Of course, more recently, Oprah made some negative comments about that same industry, was sued, but prevailed, and has apparently not suffered at all. However, Oprah is Oprah.

In the NFL, we watched talented quarterback Jim McMahon turn himself into a major media star with outrageous and, to many, offensive behavior. For a brief time, it seemed like a good idea. But it also got him bounced from a championship team, the Bears, to the basement-dwelling San Diego Chargers. The San Diego media was waiting for him—they ate him up and spit him out.

In the NBA, more recently, Dennis Rodman has wandered down the same path, and it has taken him from a starring role on the world champion Bulls through LA, for a very brief, unpleasant stint on the Lakers, to the relative ignominy of the World Wrestling Federation.

A handful of years ago, the media and the public went into such a blood-frenzy when Donald Trump's marital and financial troubles surfaced that the negative publicity scared his bankers half to death and nearly toppled his entire empire. He came within a hair's breadth of destruction, thanks to bad PR.

Sometimes being "outrageous" works, sometimes not. But when you are offensive and get your publicity by offending people, you will generally find the backlash more destructive than the original attention was helpful. There are less radical and risky approaches . . .

HOW TO GET FAVORABLE MEDIA ATTENTION AND PUBLICITY: JOINING FORCES WITH A CHARITY

For a number of years, a business associate of mine did a fantastic job aligning his stores with the Phoenix Chapter of the Arthritis Foundation. By very actively supporting its annual telethon with fundraising activities, personnel, and his assistance, he was able to obtain a large amount of free, positive publicity on radio and television. And the contacts he made in the media through this activity have proven of continuous and frequent value in promoting the business in others ways.

On a bigger, national level, my occasional client and friend Bill Phillips, CEO of the fast-growing sports nutrition company, EAS, made news by donating the proceeds of his first book, *Body For Life*, to the Make-A-Wish Foundation. This helped gain lots of favorable media attention for Bill and his book. Which helped the book shoot up the bestseller lists. Many national companies have linked themselves to my speaking colleague General Colin Powell's nonprofit organization, America's Promise, which provides resources to help at-risk kids. A national eyeglass chain, for example, donated hundreds of thousands of pairs of glasses and free eye exams. Amongst other things, this gets them mentioned by General Powell in almost every speech he gives—yet they probably couldn't hire him as a celebrity spokesperson for all the ad money they've got.

Most charities and nonprofit organizations welcome the interest of any business owner who might assist them in their fundraising activities. You'll probably be surprised at how easy it is to get involved and how little it takes in fundraising capability to be considered a VIP by the organization, especially on a local level.

Just for example, I have a client, Rod Smith, a former NFL star, who puts on nearly a hundred football-and-character-building youth camps in cities and towns all across America every summer. On a local level, a company can be a major sponsor for as little as a few thousand dollars. That gets them plenty of name recognition, publicity, literature distributed to the kids and their parents, and the added value of doing something genuinely useful in the community. (Rod's company, Dynamic Sports, is in Scottsdale, Arizona.)

So, what can you do? With collection displays like coin cans in your place of business and special promotions, you can raise money for the charity from your customers. Take a lesson from national companies like 7-11 or Dairy Queen and the countless others that donate a penny, nickel, or dime for every so many items sold during a promotional period. With the charity's permission, you can use this in your advertising and as a lever to seek free advertising.

You can also raise funds for the charity through your own employees and their friends and relatives. Activities like bowl-a-thons, walk-a-thons, and 10K races give your employees an opportunity to get pledges of x cents per pin or per mile from their friends, then an opportunity to participate and have fun. Even a small group of ten employees who each get ten people to pledge 50¢ a pin for a bowl-a-thon can collectively raise hundreds of dollars, even a thousand dollars or more.

By running several customer/public promotions and several employee activities during the half-year prior to the charity's telethon or other major fundraising event, your business can come to the party with a donation of $5,000, $10,000, or more and be viewed as a major contributor—and all without actually taking bottom-line dollars to make a contribution. If you match that with some dollars diverted from your ad budget, you can be a major player.

A word to the wise: choose your charity carefully. A group formed to preserve historic buildings in your community might sound good until it gets into conflict with the city government's plans to plop a new industrial park on that same site, bringing 2,000 new jobs to town. A feed-the-homeless program may sound great until a few of the homeless people frequenting the soup kitchen make news by burglarizing nearby homes and parked cars.

Local chapters of recognized, reputable national organizations like the Arthritis, Leukemia, or Easter Seals foundations are usually safe, and do provide a useful collection of benefits to their respective constituencies.

For your self-interest, you'll want to choose an organization that is highly visible in your community and very aggressive and progressive in its promotional activities. Frankly, there's no point in clutching the coattails of someone who's not going anywhere. An organization that has a locally *televised* telethon, auction, rodeo, or other major activity is ideal.

For the benefit of others, I encourage you to choose an organization with a policy of low overhead and high pass-through of funds in ways that genuinely help ill, handicapped, or disadvantaged people. There are unfortunately a number of nonprofits that use up most of their money on bureaucratic overhead, salaries, and fundraising rather than doing anything with it that genuinely helps people. You should also try to find an activity or organization you honestly feel is making an important contribution to society, so you get some psychic reward from your support and can create employee morale and customer loyalty with sincere enthusiasm for the cause you all join in supporting. (Personally, I've long been a supporter of Habitat for Humanity, which builds housing for the poor but insists that the recipients contribute "sweat equity.")

HOW TO GET FAVORABLE MEDIA ATTENTION AND PUBLICITY: BY BEING A FLAMBOYANT CHARACTER

Yes, there are great risks here—notably the danger of crossing the line from flamboyant to offensive, á la Trump and Helmsley in business, Andrew Dice Clay in comedy, etc. However there are great examples of this gamble paying off big, one of which is a big gambler, Bob Stupak, who created the Vegas World Hotel and Casino in Las Vegas (now the Stratosphere).

Bob has appeared on *60 Minutes*—in a positive way—been written about in many major newspapers and magazines, and hit the national wire services as news at least twice that I know of. His paths to publicity have included inventing and promoting weird casino games, like crapless craps; playing high-stakes poker against a computer; making the largest known bet on a boxing match at a competing casino—and winning; installing the world's largest wheel of fortune; and challenging Donald Trump to a huge wager on one round of the toystore product *Trump—The Game* (an offer Trump declined).

In the sports world, most people agree that Bill Veeck was the most flamboyant promoter. He's widely credited with inventing "Bat Day" for baseball, but best remembered for sending a midget up to the plate in a major league game—thus presenting the pitcher with a strike zone so small as to require surgical precision.

Cal Worthington, a California car dealer, provided late night TV in his area with truly entertaining commercials, gained national renown, and inspired a host of imitators with his circus animal commercial guest stars, Roy Roger-ish outfits, and wild promises like, "If you can beat our price, I'll eat a bug!"

In our market area, there's a dentist who, once a week, dresses up in a Superman costume and visits school health classes as "Super Dentist," along with fantastic props like an 8-foot-long toothbrush. Every so often, this flamboyant approach to community service gets him newspaper or TV coverage.

If you want a great case study, take a close look at Jesse Ventura.

By the time you read this book, he may be the most popular governor ever elected in Minnesota, contemplating a run at the White House, or he may have stepped in a mudhole that's consumed him. But right at this moment, he's riding high. Here's a former pro wrestler who ran as a Reform Party candidate in a relatively conservative state, Minnesota, and shocked both the Republican and Democratic candidates by beating them soundly. In short order, Jesse did engineer the largest tax cut and rebate in the state's history. His rather quickly written and published autobiography, *Ain't Got Time to Bleed*, made it to the top of the bestseller lists, as Jesse was everywhere: Leno, Letterman, Larry King, etc. And, well, it'd be hard to be more flamboyant than Jesse "The Body" Ventura.

HOW TO GET FAVORABLE MEDIA ATTENTION AND PUBLICITY: BY BEING AN EXPERT

The media loves surveys, polls, and statistics. If you commission or conduct some kind of public-opinion or customer-preference study, it'll probably lead to your choice of public media or trade journal exposure for you and your business. A client of mine in the time-management seminar business conducted a survey of top executives from 500 companies, asking them to rate their biggest time-management and productivity problems. Then he compiled the results into a news release and sent it to a variety of magazines, newspapers, and talk shows. He received write-ups in his local newspaper and two business magazines and was interviewed on one radio talk show. Who can copy this idea?

Couldn't a restaurant owner do a survey of dining out and take-home eating habits? Couldn't a florist compile interesting, maybe even humorous data and examples of why men buy roses?

Another certain source of media attention is issuing predictions. Being provocative and predictive attracts the media spotlight as if you were magnetized. One of our major banks gets tremendous media attention each January when it issues its "economic forecast" for the Phoenix economy in the year ahead.

About eight or nine years ago, I consulted with a group involved in the production of a TV infomercial featuring Joan Quigley, best known (as mentioned earlier) as Nancy Reagan's astrologer. I was in a board room with a group of pretty high-powered executives and creative types, working under time pressure to agree on a long list of details about the planned show, but when a brief, casual conversation started Joan talking about predictions, I can tell you that everybody's ears perked up, the clock watching was forgotten, and we, too, wanted to know—"What does Joan say?" (the title of her book about consulting with the Reagans). People are tirelessly fascinated with predictions!

Last year the radio talk shows were heavily populated with "experts" issuing their predictions about the impending Y2K crisis—and publicizing everything from books to seminars to freeze-dried potato rinds to hideouts in Montana. Being an expert making predictions is one path to lots of free radio time. There are others, which we'll discuss in a minute.

HOW TO GET FAVORABLE MEDIA ATTENTION AND PUBLICITY: WITH CREATIVE PROMOTIONS

Do you remember the pet rock? As you'll recall, that strange little product got talked about on thousands of radio stations, shown on TV, and written up in newspapers and magazines, providing its inventor with millions of dollars of free advertising. He simply sent pet rocks to the media, and they went nuts over it! On a smaller scale, you can generate media interest and coverage with your own unusual products or promotions.

The Home Club, a wholesale membership store, used a brochure made to look like a rock in a direct-mail campaign to solicit new members. Sticking with the rock theme, the club talked about its "rock bottom prices" and their location that was "only a stone's throw away," and offered, as a free gift to new members, a phony rock with a well in it to hide a spare key. The mailing pulled a remarkable 7 percent response. But the promotion was so unique it was written up in *Target Marketing Magazine* (7/90) and mentioned on local talk radio.

On a Friday the 13th, a record store erected a "superstition obstacle course" in its parking lot—complete with a ladder to walk under, a sidewalk crack to step on, mirrors to break, and a black cat roaming around—and sent dares to all the local radio disc jockeys, newspaper columnists, and TV personalities to go through the obstacle course. One radio station bit and did a live remote morning drive-time broadcast from the site. Two TV news programs reported it. Thousands of dollars of free advertising resulted.

One of our local banks has all its tellers come to work in costumes on Halloween—and for three years in a row, they've garnered free advertising on TV news programs with this gimmick.

One of my favorite publicity stunt stories is about a promotion my friend Gary Halbert devised for Tova Borgnine, for the promotion of a new perfume. They ran a big ad (headlined: "Tova Borgnine Swears Under Oath Her New Perfume Contains No Illegal Sexual Stimulants") and offered free samples to the public at a huge "premiere party" at a Los Angeles hotel. The resulting traffic jam and frenzied crowd turned the shamelessly promotional event into a news story that made the TV news, radio news, and the retailing industry news.

The "queen of publicity stunts" is Raleigh Pinskey, a publicist and consultant in—where else—Los Angeles. Raleigh has created publicity "events" for everything from the most expensive Barbie doll ever offered to the public to more ordinary, mundane businesses. I recommend her book, *101 Ways to Promote Your Business*, to everyone.

HOW TO GET FREE ADVERTISING: AS A GUEST ON RADIO TALK SHOWS

In your area, there are probably a couple of "all talk" radio stations plus other stations with at least one or two talk shows on their daily or weekly schedule. Nationally, there are tens of thousands of such stations. These shows grind up guests at a rapid pace. Their hosts and producers are constantly scrambling to find interesting guests. And there aren't nearly enough celebrities to go around. In fact, 90 percent of all radio talk show guests are ordinary people, virtually unknown to the listening audience before their appearance.

Just about anything we've talked about in this Step can qualify you as a radio talk show guest: an opinion, a prediction, a survey, a study, an opinion poll, a new product, an outrageous promotion, or a charitable activity.

Writing a book or article is an even surer path to the talk-show microphone. My friend Joe Sabah has written and self-published a little book about how to get a job and has booked himself as a guest on hundreds of radio talk shows all across the country, being interviewed over the phone from his own home, to promote his book. Lots of people could emulate his example. If you have a national chain of restaurants, you could write a book, booklet, or article about dining out while on a diet—and do radio talk shows everywhere, promoting your book and your restaurant chain free. If you have a mail-order company with a catalog of educational games for children, you could write a book, booklet, or article about raising superintelligent kids—and then be on hundreds of radio talk shows promoting your book and your catalog. Joe Sabah has done so well with this approach he's created a whole how-to manual about it and a mailing list of the best radio stations.*

And, if you can't write, you can find a ghost writer or co-author to help you, probably right in your own area. A directory of freelance writers is available from the National Writers Club, or a simple classified ad in your local paper will bring freelance writers and editors rushing to your door.

---

*For information about Joe Sabah's manual on getting on radio talk shows and mailing lists of talk shows and other media, visit *www. dankennedy.com.*

THE BASIC TOOLS FOR GETTING FREE ADVERTISING: THE PRESS KIT AND THE NEWS RELEASE

A press kit is a folder or booklet of basic information about you, your business, product, or service, your qualifications as an expert, and your background that can be universally used with any media contact as well as bankers, lenders, investors, vendors, even clients or customers. It will typically include some or all of the following:

1. A biographical sketch and/or resume.
2. A chronological history of your industry and your business, product, or service.
3. Photos of the business, product, or service.
4. Photos of you in action with your product or service; you with famous people; you being interviewed on TV, etc.
5. Copies of any articles or excerpts from books you've written.
6. Copies of articles about you and your business, product, or service.
7. Position statements or press releases—such as those about studies, surveys, polls, new products, nonprofit affiliations, awards received, etc.
8. A list of subjects on which you can be called to comment as a qualified expert.

This press kit can be sent with a cover letter to every radio station producer or manager, every TV station producer or manager, every newspaper editor, every magazine editor, individual show hosts and producers, and individual columnists. Your cover letter may suggest a particular reason to schedule you as a guest now or, more generally, suggest that your press kit be kept on file and that you be called on when they need an expert from your field. Then, periodically, you should mail new information to this same list of targets.

This is usually your first contact with a list you've compiled of media targets who might be interested in you and who could be useful to you. If you become known to these contacts as an interesting, knowledgeable source of information, you will get opportunities!

The other basic tool is a good press release. You can create one press release after another, linking yourself or your business to timely events. Best of all, press releases can be sent via broadcast-fax to radio stations and other media at nominal cost.

The world expert in using press releases successfully is my speaking colleague, Dr. Paul Hartunian.* Paul is the man who actually did sell the Brooklyn Bridge—well, little hunks of it anyway, to the tune of hundreds of thousands of dollars, all via interviews and an 800 number, all created by press releases. For that and other products and businesses, he has been on *The Tonight Show, Oprah, Sally Jesse Raphael,* on CNN, even profiled in *Forbes* magazine. He has generated literally millions of dollars of free yet valuable advertising via faxed press releases.

---

*Dr. Paul Hartunian offers a complete publicity kit, seminars on the subject, and publishes a monthly newsletter about getting publicity. For information, visit *www.dankennedy.com*.

7

MALIBUISM— BECOMING HOT

FADS AND TRENDS

Shortly after moving to Arizona in 1978, I went through a divorce, and found myself single and "in the market"—and at that time, the market was Thursday, Friday, and Saturday nights at one place and one place only: an incredibly popular nightclub called Bogart's. Anybody who was anybody frequented Bogart's. All the beautiful people frequented Bogart's. In a city of three-quarters of a million people, there might as well have been only one nightclub. The line to get in the front door was often a hundred people long, but if you "knew somebody" you could be granted the great and glorious privilege of buying a $100 membership card entitling you to enter via standing in the line at the back door, which was often shorter.

I was there on a Thursday night when it was as I've just described. But that same Saturday, I returned to find a nearly empty Bogart's. "What happened?" I asked the bartender. "Did they drop the bomb and forget to tell me?"

He shrugged his shoulders and said, "When you're hot you're hot, when you're not you're not."

Bogart's never got hot again. Only a short time later, it ceased to exist. You can sure go from hot to cold in a hurry.

ULTIMATE MARKETING SIN #3
TAKING YOUR CUSTOMER'S LOYALTY
FOR GRANTED

The entire American automobile industry nearly put itself out of business by stubbornly, stupidly *assuming* that Americans wouldn't buy Japanese cars. Network TV has lost one-third of its viewers and is now frantically trying to recover; the people who run it sat around and said, people will never pay to watch better TV programming.

Once upon a time there was buy-American loyalty. There was brand-name loyalty. There was neighborhood-merchant loyalty. Once upon a time. Today, you've got to keep getting hot all over again.

California may very well be the fad capital of America. Consider the rising and falling fortunes of EST and primal scream therapy . . . women's underwear becoming outerwear for disco nights . . . Spagos . . . the Beverly Hills Diet . . . the cellular phone . . . injections of sheep sperm. Malibu-ites can afford to indulge their every whim—they have plenty of 'em—and some whim-satisfiers make fortunes for their creators.

But California has no exclusive on all this. Tragically, young boys in all the inner cities of America have been assaulted, mugged, and occasionally even killed by others desperate for their designer-name sneakers. Even in Kansas, Austin Powers was BIG. Malibu-ism invades even Tupelo.

THE FATHER OF THE FAD
EVERYBODY REMEMBERS

On April Fool's Day, 1975, advertising man Gary Dahl dropped into his favorite tavern for a beer, got involved with a group talking about their pets, and, when asked if he had a pet, replied: "You bet. I've got a pet that's perfectly housebroken, cheap to feed, loyal, and easy to take care of and that knows tricks. In fact, he can roll over and play dead better than any other pet in the world."

"Yeah? What kind of pet is that?"

"My pet rock," Gary said, and the group broke into laughter. Pretty soon, the group was enthusiastically involved in coming up with all the best things about having a pet rock. Gary listened. Then he went home and spent a couple weeks at the typewriter coming up with the funny owner's manual to go with the pet rock.

One year later, Gary was a bona fide millionaire.

Since then, thousands of people have sought fast wealth through inventing fads; few have been successful. But a surer path to wealth is to adopt the principles behind the incredible success of the pet rock to ordinary products, services, or businesses . . . over and over and over again.

THE NEW, SHORT PRODUCT LIFE CYCLES

In an interview in *Success Magazine* (9/86), Ken Hakuta, known as "Dr. Fad," raised the issue of short product life cycles—which I prefer to call "short customer interest cycles." Ken made his first fortune in 1982, with the sticky-footed, wall-climbing octopus toys called WallWalkers. He sold nearly 150 million of those goofy things. Ken has his MBA from Harvard, but he's never been a traditional marketer. In the *Success* interview, he advised, "Pretend you're marketing to kids. They get bored with products easily and outgrow them. A company must constantly develop new ideas and be agile enough to turn them into working products—fast."

Ken observed that today's adults are acting more like kids than they used to. He astutely recognized the marketplace impact of declining attention spans and abbreviated interest cycles. This is truer than ever. These days, people have the attention span of gnats.

This behavioral trend has been helped along by the little device known as the remote control. And the trend is most easily observed while watching anybody with a remote watching TV. What do they do? You bet: click up and down, up and down, station to station. Bore them for even a second and they're gone!

It might interest you to know that men zap about four times more than women, and, conversely, women are four times more likely to click to a program and then stay there until the end than are men. This may be wired in. It's possible that males are born with an attention deficit disorder gene women don't have. It is activated by wedding vows, then stimulated repeatedly by the insertion of any small object into the hand. To any women reading: the next time he dozes off in front of the tube, gently take the remote out of his hand, gently replace it with a flashlight; when he awakes, he'll click away for five or 10 minutes before figuring out the problem!

Actually, my theory is: this little clicker is the last thing we men have any control over in the household, so by God, we're gonna use it.

Anyway, that noise you hear in a quiet neighborhood at night ain't crickets! According to research reported in the American Marketing Association Newsletter back in 1990, the average viewer "zapped" the TV once every 3 minutes, 42 seconds all night long. More recent research I'm privy to, thanks to my work in the infomercial business, indicates a "zap factor" of 2-minute cycles. This says two things: first, that the public patience is disintegrating. Two, you've got to keep "re-interesting" that viewer every 1 minute 59 seconds.

This is sort of like the "pull 'em back in" factor I talk about in the companion book to this one (*The Ultimate Sales Letter*) with regard to printed marketing materials.

This extends from the living room and TV, to the sales letter in the mail, to the Web site on the Internet, to the aisle in the store. Your customers are impatient, easily bored "zappers."

HOW NOT TO GET ZAPPED

Possibly the biggest underlying secret to Gary Dahl's Pet Rock was fun. Everybody had fun with it. It wasn't the rock; it was the idea—carried out in the owner's manual—that made it all fun.

Ken Hakuta told *Success*: "Colgate came out with a toothpaste pump first, and Crest had to play follow-the-leader. But who's to say that the pump is any better than the tube? The important thing is that it's different. In my fad marketing strategy, the pump would be only the first of many changes. A year later I might introduce different flavors; after that, toothpaste dispensed from an aerosol can; then a bubble gum toothpaste . . . well, you get the idea."

You bet—the idea is:

ULTIMATE MARKETING SECRET WEAPON #9
CONSTANT CHANGE

We are so interested in the new and different, we express it in vernacular. When we greet someone, we say, "What's *new*?" We *don't* ask, "Hey, what's old? What's the same as it was the last time I ran into you?" Why don't we ask that? Because we just don't care about what's old.

If you want to keep your customers, keep your customers interested, and keep getting your customers to tell others about you, you've got to keep coming up with good answers to the question, "What's new?"

During what insiders refer to as "the dark ages" after Walt's death, the Disney empire was crumbling—because there was nothing new going on. Eventually, Michael Eisner came in and recreated the magic of constant, almost frantic, certainly frenetic innovation, and the fortunes of the Disney business machine have never been brighter.

Probably the best example, though, is McDonald's. Hardly a two-week period passes without something new or something different going on at McDonald's: a new product, an incredible offer, a new game, a new free gift. "We can invent," Ray Kroc once said, "faster than the others can copy," and that they do. So should you.

SEVEN WAYS TO GET HOT AND KEEP GETTING HOT ALL OVER AGAIN

1. GET PRESTIGIOUS RECOGNITION

Chances are, your local newspaper or entertainment magazine publishes an annual or semiannual "Best of [your city's name]" issue. You have publications with columnists, radio shows with hosts, TV shows with reporters that all need to be wooed by you—they do have influence in your market! Having well-known people patronize your business and having the media talking about your business makes everybody else want to join the "in crowd."

If you market within an industry niche, rather than to the general public, there's less media, but its publishers and editors tend to be more accessible. In 1997, my client, Joe Polish of Pirahna Marketing was named "CleanFax Man Of The Year" and featured on that carpet cleaning industry trade journal's front cover in a striking double photo; Joe in a devil's cape with horns, and Joe as an angel with a halo, symbolizing his controversial reputation in the industry. The magazine featured a full-length, favorable profile. He has since made massive, profitable use of reprints of that article. But this didn't happen by happy accident. Over a couple years prior to this "recognition," Joe carefully and aggressively cultivated a very good relationship with the publisher of this magazine. He interviewed the publisher for his own monthly audiocassette series; he frequently mentioned the magazine in his own newsletter; he invited the publisher to his seminars; he even helped the publisher with a direct-mail campaign. He kept in constant touch with this publisher, occasionally calling just to swap ideas.

2. NEW PRODUCTS

Voraciously read trade magazines, business magazines, and newspapers—and frequently attend conventions, expos, and trade shows in search of interesting, exciting new products you can offer to your customers.

3. NEW SERVICES

Find new, different, and better ways to be of service to your customers.

4. TIE INTO TRENDS AND NEWS EVENTS

Get involved with what people are thinking and talking about. One of the great direct-response copywriters of all time, Robert Collier, talked about "entering the conversation already taking place in the prospect's mind." This is a powerful strategy, requiring considerable insight and understanding of your market, awareness of what's going on in their lives and in the news, and opportunistic action.

When Bill Gates came under attack by the government for monopolistic, unfair business practices, and every day's news was reporting on that, one of my clients alertly added copy to his ads, sales letters, and faxes talking about how using his product would give your business such an unfair advantage you'd destroy and dominate your competitors just like Bill Gates, but without having to testify or pay huge fines. Response to his advertising went up by nearly 50 percent.

Shortly after the first election of Bill Clinton, when Hillary was put in charge of the national health care scheme, it was easy to demonize her amongst conservatives. In one client's full-page magazine ad for a financial opportunity, I added a "P.S." paragraph just mentioning Hillary coming to take away a lot of your money to pay for everybody else's cradle to grave health care, and suggested that you needed to get rich fast, before it was too late— the response to the ad increased significantly.

When Desert Storm was ending, I noticed an article in a trade journal reporting on a surge in Frederick's of Hollywood's sales apparently stimulated by soldiers' wives' and girlfriends' preparations for homecoming celebrations. I clipped it and sent it to an acquaintance of mine who owns two lingerie stores in a "military town." She did a quick welcome-home theme mailing announcing a special sale to her customer list as well as to a rented list of military households, and got huge response.

5. TIE INTO SEASONS AND HOLIDAYS

Again, get involved with what people are thinking and talking about! Here's a partial list of seasons and special days you might tie a promotion to:

January/Week 1	New Years
January/Week 3	Martin Luther King Day
January/Week 4	Australia Day

February/Week 1	Start promoting for Valentine's Day
February/Week 2	Lincoln's Birthday
February/Week 3	Washington's Birthday
March/Weeks 1-3	St. Patrick's Day
March/Week 3 or 4	Spring officially begins
April/Week 1	April Fool's Day
April/Weeks 2 and 3	Easter
April/Week 4	Italian Liberation Week
May/Weeks 1-3	Mother's Day
May/Week 3	Armed Forces Day
May/Week 5	Memorial Day
June/Week 3	Flag Day
June/Week 4	Summer officially begins
	Father's Day
July/Week 1	Fourth of July
July/Weeks 2-4	Peak of summer—
	all summer activities
August/Weeks 3, 4 and 5	Back-to-School readiness
September/Week 1	Labor Day
September/Weeks 4 and 5	Rosh Hashanah, Yom Kippur
September/Week 5	Autumn officially begins
October/Week 2	Columbus Day
October/Weeks 3, 4 and 5	Halloween
November/Weeks 1 and 2	Election Day
November/Week 3	Veterans Day

November/Weeks 1,2 and 3   Thanksgiving

November/Weeks 3 and 4   Inauguration of holiday shopping season

December/All Weeks   Christmas and Hanukkah

Winter Activities

December/Weeks 3 and 4   New Year's Eve

As you can see, there's hardly a week that goes by that you can't be starting, in the throes of, or winding up a seasonal or holiday-related promotion for your business. You can also find lists of obscure holidays in books at the library or bookstore, if a lighter, humorous touch is appropriate for your business.

6. TIE INTO MOVIES AND ENTERTAINMENT EVENTS

Is a big-name entertainer or music group coming to your city? Is your baseball, football, or basketball team going into the playoffs? Does your business have some natural similarity to a currently popular movie?

You may remember the popular TV show *Twin Peaks*—with the FBI agent who loved his doughnuts. At the show's peak, I saw a doughnut shop advertising a "Twin Peaks Party Pack"—a special price for two dozen doughnuts and a chance to enter a "Guess Who Killed Laura Palmer Contest." There was a sharp proprietor who's having fun with his customers, the public, and his advertising!

The fast food chains, led by McDonalds, understand this idea very well, and pay huge sums of money for rights to link promotions to hit movies. When the second *Austin Powers* movie came out and was an instant, blockbuster hit, Richard Branson, savvy promoter at Virgin Airways, Virgin Records, etc., had heavy tie-ins with the Austin Powers character. What these giant firms pay big money to do, you can do for a smaller business, carefully and cleverly, for free. One of my Inner Circle Members sent me a copy of a sales letter he sent out for his industrial parts company, written after he saw the *Austin Powers* movie, headlined "Maybe You Need a Bigger Tool, Baby!"

7. PIGGYBACK ON OTHERS' FADS, EVEN IF UNRELATED

I don't know about you, but if they had come to me and invited me to invest in a movie about giant turtles who lived in the sewers, ate pizza, sang rock music, and were martial arts experts, I would have whipped my checkbook right out. Sure. Nevertheless, the *Teenage Mutant Ninja Turtles* were big, big, big! And Pizza Hut astutely latched onto their coat-ta, uh, shells.

But Pizza Hut didn't not own this opportunity. A dentist I know went out and bought some stuffed Teenage Mutant Ninja Turtles, displayed them in his office, and mailed all his patients this offer: bring in any child for a special $9.95 exam and he or she can take home the turtle of his or her choice—while supplies last—free!

If I had owned a pet store, a record store, a toy store, a kids' shoe store—I can guarantee you that I would have run some kind of green promotion the year the Turtles got hot.

Fortunately, there's some kind of comparable fad every few months or so. Again, some astute big companies pay attention to this. Recently, "swing" came back with a vengeance, and The Gap stores put some very effective TV ads on the air linking themselves to "swing." Every business, large or small, has similar opportunities.

"POOR BOY" MARKETING STRATEGIES

GETTING CUSTOMERS WITHOUT GOING BROKE

Early in my business career, I was wisely advised, "Boy, the first thing you gotta do is avoid going broke while you're getting rich and famous." Had I paid closer attention, I might very well have saved myself from considerable financial strife. Observing others, I've noticed how frequently entrepreneurs bankrupt themselves with expensive advertising and marketing schemes when their interests would be better served by low-cost methods. When you stop to think about it, it's easy to "buy customers"—given enough money (or credit), any idiot can build up a business, and many idiots have, using up millions of dollars of stockholders' equity in the process. Genius is in getting customers and making sales without having to use up a huge chunk of capital to do it. The ideas in this chapter are dedicated to that objective.

IT'S OPPORTUNITY CALLING!

The phone rang persistently in the little shoe store where I was buying a pair of shoes. Finally, after six rings, the clerk at the counter said, "Dammit—I'm busy," but grudgingly answered the phone. Guess how he sounded to the caller?

This attitudinal error must occur a million times a day in every imaginable type of business, as the incoming call "interrupts" the important work. Fix this and you've taken a giant step forward in attracting new customers as well as retaining the ones you have.

An inbound call can be many things: the tax collector, your mother-in-law announcing a surprise two-week visit, or the merchant next door reporting that your roof is on fire. These calls have varying degrees of importance. But the call can be and often is from a prospective customer, present customer, or past customer, and that is Opportunity calling! These calls must not be thought of as interruptions.

If the call is from a prospective customer, the job of the person handling the call must be clearly defined, understood, and enthusiastically pursued: to get the customer into the store or to get her name, address, and phone number, or to set up an appointment. It is not just to dispense information.

Let me tell you one of the most instructive true marketing stories I have ever encountered:

> The owner of a large auto-parts store was extraordinarily frustrated with his advertising, complaining about weekly expenditures of tens of thousands of dollars in the newspaper, on radio, and on television, all yielding few customers. But a conversation with his employees revealed their frustration with the constant ringing of the phone—calls from people asking questions, constantly interrupting them. A Saturday in his store provided a count of over 200 incoming calls. Here's how every one was handled, with varying levels of courtesy and friendliness:

> "XYZ Auto Parts—how can we help you?" The caller would then state his business. Most often, his inquiry sounded like this: "I saw [heard] your ad—how much is a flibittygibbet for a '68 Ford?"

> The answer then went like this: "Lemme look it up—hold on . . . still there? It's sixty-two fifty." Click.

As you can immediately detect, there was no problem at all with this guy's advertising. And, to be fair, his people really weren't at fault either. He was the problem. He was the one who had no earthly idea what was going on inside his own business. He was the one who had failed to educate his people about the importance of these calls. He was the one who had failed to train his people in effective handling of the calls. He was the one who had failed to motivate his people. He was the one who had failed to monitor their performance.

Here's what we did:

1. We devised a new phone script to capture the caller's name, address, and number.

2. We taught the script to all the employees.

3. We instituted a reward pool of 50 cents per captured name, address, and phone number, divided at day's end by everybody working that day.

4. We added a "telephone upsell" to the script.

ULTIMATE MARKETING SECRET WEAPON #10
CAPTURE CALLERS' IDENTITY
AND MARKET TO THEM

Immediately, with this strategy, the number of callers converted, ones who came into the store that same day, increased significantly. Overall, after follow-up mailings to all the callers, the store captured over 50 percent of the callers as customers!

ULTIMATE MARKETING SECRET WEAPON #11
THE TELEPHONE UPSELL

In addition, we added revenue and profit with the telephone upsell.

You're familiar with this if you've ever ordered by phone from a well-run catalog company. After the operator has taken your order, she'll usually do a "Columbo": "Oh, just one more thing . . . we have a special offer just for today's callers—would you like to hear about it?" I recently ordered from The Sharper Image, and the operator walked me through six different specials.

This technique works in that application, and there's no reason it can't work in others.

The auto-parts store's upsell script sounded like this:

"Oh, just one more thing—we have an extra special offer just for today's callers—would you like to hear about it?"

Over 70 percent said yes.

"Good. Any caller who comes in today or by noon tomorrow will receive a five percent discount coupon good for any purchase in the store and a free copy of our four-hundred-page catalog. Also, there's a sale right now on [insert product]. I can set your coupon and catalog aside in your name if you are coming in. Should I do that?"

Over 50 percent said yes. Over 25 percent actually showed up. Over 15 percent came in, bought the item they originally called to ask about, and bought the sale item described on the phone.

REACH OUT AND GRAB
A CUSTOMER

Fact: the telephone lines run in both directions, in and out. According to Bernie Goldberg, author of the book *How to Manage and Execute Telephone Selling*, someone making outbound tele-marketing calls to homes can average 25 to 35 dialings per hour and 10 to 15 completed calls per hour; someone calling busi-nesses, 20 to 30 dialings and 5 to 10 completed calls per hour. If a person costs you $5 per hour and completes just 5 calls, that's a cost of $1 per presentation; if the person gets 10 done, you're down to a cost of 50¢ per presentation. This is comparable to or less than other advertising and marketing methods and much faster to get done.

Why the telephone? Well, just about everybody's got one. And just about everybody answers it when it rings. They may skip your ad in the newspaper. They may throw out your mail unopened. But when the phone rings, they answer.

My appreciation for the phone goes back to age 15 (yes—15!) when I decided to make some money selling Amway products. My parents were distributors, and I have to say, as an aside, that the exposure to selling, to certain attitudes, and to ambitious people that I got, thanks to their involvement, was and is priceless.

Having no money with which to advertise and no car with which to get around in and no friends, relatives, or neighbors to sell to—those were my parents' customers—I was left with the telephone and the White Pages. With some help, I devised a little telephone survey beginning with questions about environmental and water-pollution concerns, then switching to a pitch for Amway's biodegradable, ecologically wonderful, etc., laundry compound. Even the fuzziness of the passing of time has not blurred the memory of how miserable it was to make these calls:

hundreds and hundreds of no answers, hundreds of people too old, too young, unable to speak English, or unbelievably nasty, and hours without a positive response. But I also clearly remember the "thrill of victory." And, more important, I can look back and realize that with a lousy script, terrible technique, and no selectivity in prospects, I still made money and acquired customers. I long ago left that business, but I happen to know that some of those customers are still buying Amway products today, month after month after month, each having cumulatively spent tens of thousands of dollars.

There are smarter ways to use telemarketing than that, but there are worse ways to acquire customers, too.

For a printing company, I had a list compiled of small businesses and phone numbers from the area immediately surrounding the shop, created a simple phone script, and made a competition out of it for the five employees, none of whom were salespeople or telemarketers. They each "found the time" to make one call per hour, eight calls a day. The one who got the most new customers during the week got $100. The shop made 40 calls a day, 200 calls a week for $100—50¢ each. The shop also gained an average of 10 new customers each week. ANY business could copy this idea.

Some years ago, Fran Tarkenton, former NFL superstar turned businessman, with whom I had the pleasure of co-authoring *The Be Your Own Boss System* for *Entrepreneur Magazine* and with whom I've worked on two TV infomercials, got the idea of selling advertising space on airline ticket jackets. He struck a deal with an airline, then faced a question: How best to get the advertisers under contract?

Fran chose the simplest, cheapest, fastest way he could think of. He locked himself in a New York City hotel room for several days and called prospects on the phone. The strength of his name was enough to get through to decision-makers; other marketers have to find other ways to get that done. In less than a week, Fran sold millions of dollars of advertising contracts for his newly invented medium to major national corporations and made himself a lot of money.

There is one overwhelmingly superior way most businesses should use telemarketing, if they use it only one way:

ULTIMATE MARKETING SECRET WEAPON #12
TELEMARKETING AFTER DIRECT MAIL

Almost without exception, a telemarketing campaign linked to direct mail increases the initial direct-mail results by 500 to 1000 percent!

Here's a formula for a telemarketing script that is simple and effective:

1. IDENTIFY YOURSELF
This is John Smith from ABC Widgets calling.

2. REASON FOR CALLING
I'm calling to arrange for delivery of a free gift for the person in your company responsible for purchasing widgets.
OR
I'm calling to follow-up on my letter to the person in charge of purchasing widgets, to arrange for delivery of his free gift.

3. IDENTIFY DECISION-MAKER
Who in your company handles widget purchasing?

4. GET TO THE DECISION-MAKER
May I speak to Mr. Widget Buyer for just three minutes please?

5. GET PAST "SCREENING"
Rather than leaving my name and number, I'd very much appreciate setting a time that I should call back—I need to arrange for delivery of his gift with him personally within two days. (ALTERNATIVE CLOSE) Would it be better if I called back at [insert time] or [insert time]?

6. REPEAT 1 AND 2 WITH DECISION-MAKER
Mr. Widget Buyer, I'm John Smith from ABC Widgets. As part of our [insert month] new-customer promotion, your company has been selected to receive, as a free gift, [insert whatever the gift is] just for [insert desired result: coming in to store this week, setting up an appointment, whatever] and I'm calling to arrange for you to receive this gift.

7. ASK FOR THE DESIRED ACTION
Example: I'd like to personally bring your gift in and give you a brief demonstration of the ABC Widget in action. Would tomorrow morning or afternoon be better for you?
OR
Example: I'd like to set your gift aside with your name on it, but I have to know when you'll be coming in. Will tomorrow morning or afternoon be better for you?

YCDBSOYA

My father has a pair of cufflinks—he's had them since I was a kid and first asked about them—they're black squares with raised gold letters: YCDBSOYA. The letters stand for:

You Can't Do Business Sitting On Your Ass

A few years ago, a favorite restaurant of mine failed during its "summer slump." But at no time did its owners get up off their butts and go out into the community door to door to hand out coupons or flyers. Or go to the phone and make telemarketing calls. Or do anything else that was proactive. They just sat there and died.

In the same community, that same summer, a young chiropractor got ready to open his new practice—with at least a dozen competing chiropractors surrounding his office already established in the area. He spent one full month prior to opening going door to door, house to house, introducing himself, asking the residents about the area and their health interests, and making friends. He knocked on over 2000 doors that month. And from the first day he started seeing patients, his practice has prospered. Its first year it out-performed all the established practices in the area.

There are three types of people: those who *make* things happen, those who *watch* things happen, and those who *wonder* what happened. I think you'll find that most successful business-people you know are in the first category.

THE POWER OF COOPERATION

Cooperation can be carried too far, a camel being a horse built by committee, and I am not a big fan of groups. But I do believe in strategic alliances.

ULTIMATE MARKETING SECRET WEAPON #13
ASSET SHARING FOR MARKETING SUCCESS

Two noncompeting but somehow related merchants—a pet store owner and a veterinarian; a restaurant owner and a theater owner; a sporting goods store owner and a sports-bar proprietor; an auto dealer and a carwash owner; a computer company and an office supply store—can share their customer bases, their store traffic, even their advertising in order to build each others' businesses and in order to stretch their advertising dollars.

THROUGH THE LOOKING GLASS

Bruce David, a savvy marketing consultant, told me about the hardware storeowner located in a busy shopping center. The owner white-painted almost all of his window, leaving open only a small circle that passersby could look through. Above the circle, he posted a sign reading FOR MEN'S EYES ONLY.

Inside, Bruce and the storeowner had constructed an impressive display of power tools along with signs featuring great sale prices.

As you can imagine, people lined up to peer through the circle. Very few people passed without looking. People who would have passed an ordinary window display without a second glance were drawn to this display. And, in case you were wondering, just as many women looked as did men.

If you own any kind of retail establishment and can't "steal" this idea, you're braindead. I am continually amazed at the number of businesspeople who do not use their windows to promote and to attract customers.

Here are some other great window ideas:

- "Live" mannequins
- Big-screen TVs playing videos
- Weird objects, like The World's Largest Ball of Barbed Wire
- Huge objects. A company in New York called THINK BIG, INC. offers giant pencils, crayons, toothbrushes, baseball gloves, and dozens of other objects perfect for store-window displays.

TEASER ADVERTISING

The problem with running a big ad in the newspaper, in a trade journal, or in a national magazine is the number of people you pay for who simply don't see it. On any one day, your best prospects may be out of town, sick in bed, or too busy to read the newspaper.

One strategy to focus attention on your big ad is to precede it with a series of tiny, low-cost teaser ads. For example, consider the new computer store desirous of making the business community aware of its existence. For two months, in the weekly city business journal, it ran these small display ads:

COMING ON THIS PAGE IN 4 WEEKS:

THE MOST ADVANCED . . .

COMING ON THIS PAGE IN 3 WEEKS:

THE MOST ADVANCED SOLUTIONS . . .

COMING ON THIS PAGE IN 2 WEEKS:

THE MOST ADVANCED SOLUTIONS TO 46 DIFFERENT . . .

COMING ON THIS PAGE IN JUST 1 WEEK:

THE MOST ADVANCED SOLUTIONS TO 46 DIFFERENT NAGGING, FRUSTRATING, EXPENSIVE BUSINESS PROBLEMS PLUS 1 ABSOLUTELY IRRESISTIBLE FREE GIFT OFFER . . .

By the time the computer store ran its full-page grand-opening advertisement, including suggested computer solutions to 46 problems and a great free-gift offer, the regular readers of this journal *were looking for his ad.*

TAKE-ONE BOXES AND CONTEST-ENTRY BOXES

Everything from cosmetic makeovers and spa memberships to vacation clubs and credit cards are successfully promoted via take-one boxes and contest-entry boxes placed in businesses.

The purpose of these box systems is, of course, to collect names of somewhat qualified prospects for follow-up by mail or phone. A box can cost as little as a couple of dollars and, located in a busy business, collect hundreds of leads each week. A retail business that I had an interest in for several years had its managers drop off contest entry boxes at outdoor bank ATM machines on Friday evenings and pick them up Sunday evenings to collect hundreds and hundreds of leads for telemarketing follow-up. The banks probably would not have approved of this gambit, but I will tell you, it was very effective.

A couple years ago, I worked with a company marketing home security and fire protection systems by bringing homeowners to group presentations at local restaurants, as winners of free dinners. They got all their leads from contest entry boxes placed (with permission, unlike the above mentioned guerilla use of ATM locations) in gas stations, convenience stores, other retail stores, beauty salons, etc. all over each town where they had sales reps.

If I had a business that could effectively follow up on leads by mail or phone, I would develop a contest-entry box and hire a reliable, ambitious college student in need of extra income to place a number of the boxes and then service them weekly or biweekly, and then pay the kid by the number of leads or the number of leads converted to appointments or customers.

When using a contest-entry box system, it's important to offer and honestly deliver a valuable, appealing first prize. In Phoenix, weekend getaways to cooler San Diego work very well. But, although not announced in advance, every entrant wins a second prize.

Let's say you want to promote an Italian restaurant, and you want to specifically increase your weekday early dinner traffic. First, you get 10 contest-entry boxes placed in nonrestaurant businesses, probably in a circle around your restaurant. Second, you collect all the leads after a week or two. Third, you or somebody else calls these leads or you send mail to these leads with this message:

THANK YOU FOR ENTERING OUR SAN DIEGO VACATION CONTEST. UNFORTUNATELY, YOU DID NOT WIN THE FIRST PRIZE—IT WAS WON BY MR. AND MRS. JONES OF GLENDALE, ARIZONA. HOWEVER, YOU HAVE WON A VALUABLE SECOND PRIZE: THE ENCLOSED

CERTIFICATE ENTITLES YOU AND YOUR SPOUSE OR FRIEND TO A 2-FOR-1 DINNER DEAL AT OUR BEAUTIFUL ITALIAN RISTORANTE ON 12TH STREET, MONDAY THROUGH THURSDAY FROM 5:00 TO 7:30 PM. WITH THIS CERTIFICATE, YOU PAY FOR JUST 1 DINNER AND GET A 2ND DINNER OF EQUAL OR LESSER VALUE FREE! ENCLOSED IS A MINIATURE COPY OF OUR MENU SO YOU CAN SEE IN ADVANCE THE TREMENDOUS VARIETY AND REASONABLE PRICES WE OFFER. PLEASE CALL FOR RESERVATIONS AND REDEEM YOUR CERTIFICATE WITHIN THE NEXT TWENTY-ONE DAYS.

If nothing else, these strategies dispel the damaging, often repeated idea that you need money to make money. I was recently at a seminar where each attendee's business project was analyzed, discussed, and worked on by the entire group. One fellow came there with the belief he needed to raise or borrow two million dollars to successfully implement his business project. By the time the seminar was over, he had a good business plan requiring less than $5,000.

MAXIMIZING TOTAL CUSTOMER VALUE

When you ask a group of businesspeople to list their assets, they quickly write down such items as equipment, furniture, leasehold improvements, and inventory. Many never get around to listing their customers. This lapse is often reflective of trouble in their businesses.

In every *successful* business, the customer *is*, is *perceived* as, and is *treated* as the most important asset. To really get to that point and "own" that belief, you have to figure out what your customer is worth to you and can or should be worth to you.

For a period of four or five years, I bought well over half my clothes from one store; suits, sports jackets, slacks. I'd say my average annual purchases at this store have been $4,000. In five years, I was worth $20,000 in gross. I was also responsible for bringing two business associates and one client to that store, none as good a customer as I've been, but each worth at least half that much. So let's call them $6,000 a year, total. Obviously, just as I brought them in, they each have the potential of bringing in additional customers. For the sake of example, let's use a reduced amount; let's say they'd bring in additional customers worth $1,500 a year, total.

All together, $11,500 a year . . . over $57,500 every five years.

This store lost me as a customer over this incident: A Sansabelt suit I bought there, I think for $400, was, in my opinion, defective. The fabric itself sort of rippled or pimpled after only a few wearings and dry cleanings. I brought it back and asked them to show it to their Sansabelt factory rep the next time he was in to see them, and to "work something out for me." I didn't demand anything. I left it open for them to respond to me with some kind of offer.

After a month, I dropped in. They didn't bring up the suit. I had to ask. The answer was: "Sorry—there's nothing we can do."

So, for $400 or less, they kissed off over $50,000 in the next five years. They just never thought through the math.

Today, I have a client, Bill Glazer, who owns two menswear stores in the Baltimore area (Gage Menswear) and who consults with menswear retailers all across the country. Bill very astutely has a multi-step, very assertive customer retention system in place in his stores, involving direct-mail, the assignment of an individual sales rep to each customer in an on-going relationship, and fast, generous complaint resolution. It is not coincidental that he averages a multiple of the average stores' dollars per square foot in sales, has very high, measured customer loyalty, and has withstood both the disintegration of a downtown shopping area around one of his stores and the TV ad-driven assault on his market by a giant "warehouse style" menswear chain.

Here's why businesses lose customers:

One percent die
Not much that we can do about that—if they insist on dying on us, that's sort of unpreventable and irreversible.

Three percent move away
Well, people do move. If they move quite a distance outside our market area, there's not much we can do about that, either.

Five percent follow a friend or relative's advice and switch to that friend's preferred merchant
You might be tempted to say there's nothing much to be done about that either, but I'd disagree. How come we lost our customer to his buddy's merchant instead of that other merchant losing his customer to us?

Nine percent switch due to price or a better product
Some of this nine percent can't be prevented, but I'll argue that some could. Why don't we have the best product? Or—if we do—why didn't our customer know that?

Fourteen percent switch due to product or service dissatisfaction
True—you just can't please everybody. So some of this is unavoidable, too. But it's my experience as a consumer that a lot of businesses lose me for this reason, are aware of it, but don't even make an attempt at preventing the loss, just like the clothing store I mentioned. Incredibly, they give up without a fight.

But add all that up and you've accounted for only 32% of the losses. Why do the majority of customers leave? Can you guess? Sixty-eight percent switch because of what they perceive and describe as indifference from the merchant or someone in the merchant's organization. In other words, they felt unappreciated, unimportant, taken for granted. That's not my theory, remember—that's what actual customers have said.

ULTIMATE MARKETING SECRET WEAPON #14
MAKE THE CUSTOMER FEEL IMPORTANT,
APPRECIATED, AND RESPECTED

On an impulse, a business associate of mine once deviated from our mutual habit of buying and driving Lincolns and bought a BMW—a very, very expensive automobile. The car was a lemon: air conditioning that repeatedly failed, door locks that didn't work, a bad starter, etc. But far more annoying than those things was the way the dealership treated him. Quite frankly, I've never seen anything as outrageous as this dealer's complete, callous, and utter disregard for its responsibilities to this customer. I could tell you story after story, and they all add up to one thing: a car dealer who is wholly ignorant of the concept of Total Customer Value.

Not only will my associate never buy a car there again, he's made certain that I wouldn't, he's talked at least three people seriously interested in BMWs out of going there, and he's still griping to anybody and everybody who will listen.

HOW TO DO IT RIGHT

In Montreal, next to the Lord Berri Hotel, there is a parking lot. If you stay at the hotel, you park there for a day fee, or by the hour if you're doing business in the area. It is an unpaved lot with a little ramshackle hut where the attendants sit, wait, and listen to a cheap AM radio hung on a nail. In the winter, they shiver and thaw their hands over a portable space heater; in the rain, huddle and try to dry out between customers; in the summer, they sweat, relieved only by a small electric fan.

There's nothing distinctive about this parking lot. And it's not the kind of place you expect anything above minimal service.

This particular evening, an associate and I had finished conducting a seminar in the hotel and had gone to the parking lot to retrieve our rental car to go in search of a good restaurant.

On the stool, leaning against the hut was a guy wearing a T-shirt. The Parking Lot Guy. Nothing distinctive about him, either. No different than the guys in T-shirts you might run into in any parking lot in any city in the United States or Canada. But this Parking Lot Guy is an exciting reminder that you dare not judge all books by their covers. This Parking Lot Guy should probably be running General Motors.

"Where do you gentlemen want to go with your car tonight?" he asked. We explained that we were heading for an Italian restaurant we'd found advertised in a magazine.

"No," he said, "you don't want to go there. There are much better Italian restaurants much closer, even within walking distance."

A 15 minute conversation then took place. He politely quizzed us about our preferences. He got out a telephone directory and called several restaurants to determine how late they were serving, what their specials were, even what wine they had in stock. Finally, we settled on a restaurant a few blocks away. He drew us a map and carefully gave us directions.

If this hasn't shocked you, you haven't done much traveling, and you haven't parked in many parking lots. This guy—for $7 a day to park our car—was taking better care of us than the staffs and concierges of most hotels we've stayed in, at $100, $150, or even $200 a day.

He was polite, concerned, friendly, and knowledgeable. We told him so. He said:

"That's my business; that's what I sell: I'm in the service business. If I can help a person or make friends with a person when he brings his car here the first time, then the next time he has to park his car downtown, he'll remember me and my place. He may even tell somebody else to park his or her car here. If he comes back a number of times, then I'm building a stable business. Then he's not worth a few dollars to me, he may be worth a hundred dollars to me in a year. In my lifetime, he could pay to send one of my kids to college for a year. If I have enough of that kind of customer, then I have a truly valuable business. You can't do that just by parking cars. There are hundreds of car lots. They've all got parking spaces. We have to give service."

I know that's what he said, because as soon as I got seated at the restaurant, I wrote down his words as I remembered them, while it was all fresh in my mind.

It is, I think, a sad commentary on the state of business and customer service in general in our society that the very best example I can put up on a pedestal for you to emulate is The Guy in the Parking Lot. But in my book, he wins hands-down.

THE ATTITUDE OF GRATITUDE

I think the kind of customer service that makes customers feel important, appreciated, and respected begins not as policies and procedures but, instead, as an attitude of gratitude.

I was in a doctor's office one day when he asked his receptionist, "What's our body count today?" And that's not uncommon. I've heard customers called bodies, numbers, marks, even chumps. I've seen owners and managers rage on and on about how miserable their customers are—in front of their staffs! These attitudes have to translate into actions, as all attitudes do.

Although it may sound simplistic, getting maximum total value from your customers begins with valuing them totally!

MAKE EVERYONE ON YOUR TEAM
AN AMBASSADOR OF
CUSTOMER-SERVICE DIPLOMACY

To excel in customer service, every member of your team has to understand, accept, and live it as a priority.

Is the customer always right? Surely you've heard that adage: the customer is always right. But you don't have to be in business very long before you know how totally false that is. Although they are thankfully a minority, some customers are grossly unreasonable, some virtually impossible to satisfy. Taking a "the customer is always right" approach to customer service dooms your efforts before they begin. Neither you nor the members of your team will be able to live up to that ideal. I'm not even sure that you should if you could. From time to time, there'll be a customer you will be better off without. I have occasionally "terminated" customers and clients in my businesses, I think for good cause, and always found that the vacuum quickly filled with better business.

A better, more accurate approach comes from my friend, a customer-service training expert, Frank Cooper, who says, "The customer signs your paycheck." With that in mind, we can design a Customer-Service Diplomacy Program that makes sense but doesn't force us to aspire to the unattainable.

Diplomacy is all about being gracious, sort of "old-world gracious." If you've every been to a very formal party at a very wealthy person's home, an old country club, or an embassy, you know what I mean.

Walt Disney insisted that his customers be thought of, always referred to, and treated as "guests," drawing the analogy that if you treat the customer as you would an honored guest in your home, you'll rarely err.

I'd suggest incorporating these key ideas into your own clearly defined, written, taught, and managed Customer-Service Diplomacy Program:

1. GREET THE CUSTOMER AS A WELCOME, HONORED, IMPORTANT GUEST

This means that the customer can never be an interruption. Those who answer your telephones must be professionally educated in good business telephone manners and must use them.

If you've ever walked up to a cash register in a department store and stood waiting while two sales clerks finished their conversation, you've experienced the opposite of this idea—and I'll bet you resented it.

2. BE ABLE TO ANSWER CUSTOMERS' QUESTIONS KNOWLEDGEABLY

One of the reasons for the outstanding success of The Home Depot chain of hardware, housewares, and do-it-yourself product warehouse stores is the surprising helpfulness and knowledge of their employees. Here, you get the kind of customer service found in old, sole-proprietor hardware stores, but in a modern superstore environment with discount prices.

And if you have staff members who cannot be knowledgeable experts about your products and services, then they must have a good means of immediately getting an answer for any customer at any time that the place of business is open.

This year, while "shopping" some residential communities for a client, masquerading as a customer, I asked one salesman a question like this: "If I give you a deposit today on Property A and then want to change my mind and switch it to Property B before 30 days are up, can I do that?"

The salesman honestly didn't know. He probably should have. But he didn't. And at 4:45 PM there was no one he could go to or call to get the answer. So he stalled. Had I been a real customer, this would have been the equivalent of stopping a sale dead in its tracks. (By the way, the correct answer was yes.)

3. PREVENT POLICIES FROM DRIVING AWAY CUSTOMERS

I have given up counting—I no longer know (or care) how many times I've been told, "That's our policy." In most cases, my response is, "I've got a policy, too. My policy is never to spend another nickel with your business after I've been told about your policy."

Of course you have to have policies. I run businesses; I know that. But you'd better remember this one: as a prison warden, you can make up all the policies you want to because you've got a captive audience—they can't leave. Your customer, however, has "the final option." He can put his money back in his pocket and walk away, never to return. Nothing incenses customers more than being quoted "policy."

The very best policy is to create ways to say yes to customer wants and needs. I've been in restaurants where NO SUBSTITU-TIONS is imprinted on the menu in big, bold type; where, if asked, the waitress snaps, "no separate checks." Their policy is "our way or the highway." An awful lot of basically good customers choose the highway.

4. HAVE A PROCESS FOR HANDLING COMPLAINTS IN PLACE

This is not the place to play it catch-as-catch-can. An angry, irate, unsatisfied customer on the loose in the marketplace can and often will cause you considerable damage. At the very least, each one will spread the word to a dozen or more present or potential customers. They will take dollars right out of your bank account. At worst, they may also cause you some grief with the Better Business Bureau, the Attorney General's Office, or other bureaucracies. Occasionally, a customer driven over the edge strolls in with a shotgun and does some permanent damage.

You need to have a sensible, step-by-step process decided on and in place for diplomatically handling and attempting to resolve complaints.

ULTIMATE MARKETING SIN #4
LETTING A CUSTOMER LEAVE ANGRY WITHOUT FIRST EXHAUSTING EVERY MEANS AT YOUR DISPOSAL TO RESOLVE THE DISPUTE

The foundation of maximizing total customer value has to be creative excellence in keeping and satisfying customers!

CUSTOMER RETENTION AS A PROFIT CENTER

Writing for *Success Magazine* (5/90), marketing consultant George Walther described how U.S. West Cellular's "Retention Group" has turned keeping customers into a corporate profit center.

It cost that company about $700 to get a new customer, then about seven months to recover that cost before beginning to reap profits from the relationship. But half of all the new customers were dropouts before the seventh month. Company analysts figured that cutting the monthly cancellation rate by just one-tenth of one percent would add about one million bucks to the bottom line.

An elite team, The Retention Group, was created to place "welcome calls" to new customers, explain their first bills to them, and respond to customers who wanted to discontinue service. When a Retention Group "soldier" saved a customer, he jumped up and rang a brass bell in the Group's work area. Bonuses were paid on "saves."

The results were impressive: the "save rate" for all customers who called to discontinue service improved by 150 percent, and overall monthly attrition dropped by one-third. The company accountants rate the program as worth $8 million in its first year.

Walther points out that you have about a 1-in-16 chance of making a sale to a new prospect, but a 1-in-2 shot of making a repeat or subsequent, related sale to an existent customer. It obviously makes sense to treat customer retention as a profit center.

More and more companies are catching on to this idea. In recent years, the use of comprehensive "customer retention programs" has been a topic of conversation, and a serious experiment, for many of my clients, ranging from Weight Watchers International, Inc. to giant mortgage companies to dental and chiropractic practices, tanning salons, and fitness centers. Weight Watchers core business is based on weeks; extending the average customer's participation by just one more week represents millions of dollars.

In 1997 through 1999, the mortgage industry was in a "superheated condition" thanks to low interest rates, and people were refinancing to save money at a record pace. Saving customers became more important than getting them, and each month a mortgage company was able to keep its mortgages in house equated to millions of dollars.

On a smaller scale, the local tanning center's business is built on weeks, the chiropractic practice on visits. The cost of acquiring a patient is exactly the same whether that patient comes in for four visits or 14—but the profit differential from just five versus four is substantial. There may be an unexploited profit center hidden in your business, too: customer retention!

KEEP IN TOUCH

Mary Kay Cosmetics convinced their sales force to turn in over five million customer names and addresses so the company could mail them promotional literature periodically, urging the customers to call their representatives to order. These mailings have pulled in responses as high as 33 percent!

I am amazed at how many businesses have gotten me to give them money once, twice, even several times, then never contacted me again. And, while they're ignoring me, their competitors pursue me with all of the ardor associated with the new customer.

Every business should have a customer mailing list and mail information, offers, seasonal greetings, and other materials to those customers at least six, eight, or 10 times a year.

THE FOUR WAYS TO INCREASE TOTAL CUSTOMER VALUE

There are only four ways to increase Total Customer Value:

1. INCREASE AVERAGE ORDER OR PURCHASE SIZE.
Restaurants do this by effectively merchandising desserts and take-home treats and other products. Industrial marketers do it by expanding product line use and "upping" the customer to bigger sizes. Mail-order companies do it with "today's telephone specials" offered to the caller after her intended order has been taken.

2. INCREASE FREQUENCY OF REPEAT PURCHASE.
Using rewards, discounts, frequent buyer clubs, volume rebates, and frequent contact, you can capture a larger share of each customer's expenditures.

Murray Raphael*, direct marketing expert and developer of the retail mall in Atlantic City called Gordon's Alley, says, "In

---

*Murray Raphael is the author of several outstanding books on direct marketing for retailers, and is a regular contributor to *Direct Marketing Magazine*. Information about Murray's books is available at *www.dankennedy.com*.

Gordon's Alley, we have put together a Gordon's Gold Card program. The criteria is simple: did a customer spend $1,000 a year or more with us? If they did, terrific. They are entitled to a Gold Card. Now, what does the Gold Card entitle them to? Lots of nice things, including:

1. A free lunch every month from our Alley Deli.
2. Advance announcements of sales by first-class mail.
3. Special vacation packages—a tie-in with our on-site travel agency.
4. Unadvertised specials. Every once in a while, we'll look over our stock and see we don't have enough for a full-blown sale/reduction, but enough for a select group of customers. That's you, Mr./Ms. Gold Card.
5. Free gift wrapping.
6. Birthday presents—a special gift from our in-store gourmet shop, and with it a $10 gift certificate, which brings them into our store."

Now, I want you to notice two things about Murray's brilliant program: first, it has built-in frequent contact with customers. Two, its every feature works to bring the customer back to the store. Why don't more stores and businesses do this? Why don't groups of noncompeting businesses get together and do this? I dunno.

3. OFFER EXISTENT CUSTOMERS A GREATER VARIETY OF GOODS AND SERVICES.

These people are predisposed to buy from you.

ULTIMATE MARKETING SECRET WEAPON #15
DEVELOPING NEW PRODUCTS AND SERVICES
FOR EXISTENT CUSTOMERS INSTEAD OF
GETTING NEW CUSTOMERS FOR EXISTENT
PRODUCTS AND SERVICES

4. GET EXISTENT CUSTOMERS TO BRING YOU THEIR
FRIENDS, RELATIVES, NEIGHBORS, BUSINESS ASSOCIATES,
EMPLOYEES, AND OTHERS AS NEW CUSTOMERS.
We'll explore this in detail in a later chapter. Suffice it to say for
now that referrals can be the lifeblood of a business.

10

FUELING WORD-OF-MOUTH ADVERTISING

Let's begin by recognizing that there is no better new customer than a referral from a happy customer. I don't care what business you're in, this is true. The referred customer has less skepticism and is less price-resistant, more receptive, and more easily sold and satisfied.

Most businesses take referrals for granted. Whatever number of referrals they get, they gratefully accept, but they have no proactive plan for stimulating the maximum number of referrals.

HOW MANY REFERRALS CAN YOU GET?

Joe Girard, repeatedly recognized by the *Guiness Book Of World Records,** has a "Rule of 52," based on his discovery that the average number of attendees at both weddings and funerals is 52. In marketing to consumers, his contention is that each customer has the potential of referring 52 other customers. Even if we cut his number in half, ask yourself: is your business averaging 26 referrals per customer? Probably not—most average anywhere from less than one to three. There is room for improvement.

In business-to-business marketing, the numbers are different. I did some admittedly clumsy but I think instructive research: I took executives and business owners in a dozen different industries and had them go through their trade association directories and count the number of people whom they knew (and who knew them) on a first-name basis. The average was 37— thus each business customer has the ability to refer 37 others to a vendor.

---

*Joe Girard is the author of *How to Sell Anything to Anybody*.

THE WAY TO GET REFERRALS IS WITH THE EAR FORMULA

Listen, my friends, and I'll tell you how to fuel your word-of-mouth advertising to new, unprecedented levels!

E stands for *EARN*; we have to *earn* our referrals. Walt Disney put it this way: "Do what you do so well that people can't resist telling others about you."

In my speaking career, I've been very fortunate in two ways. Since beginning in 1978, I've averaged over 70 compensated engagements each and every year until recently, when I've started deliberately cutting back, and over half of all those engagements have come from referrals—in other words, this marketing expert has done very little to market himself as a speaker! I haven't had to. Instead, I've focused on doing what I do so well that my clients are inspired to tell others about me. Also, I've gotten an incredible amount of consulting work as a direct result of these same speaking performances. For example, very recently, speaking for just 45 minutes at a conference of just 36 business owners immediately yielded six new clients and over $100,000 in new consulting business.

ULTIMATE MARKETING SECRET WEAPON #16
EXCELLENCE

If there is one "secret" to maximum referrals, it is that satisfied customers do not refer abundantly. Enthused, inspired, awed customers refer in great abundance. If you are just good enough, that's not good enough. If customers get only what they expect and deserve, that's not enough.

Let me tell you about a dentist who multiplied his practice by 10 in just one year without even a $1 increase in his advertising budget. He caters to children and, after a seminar on creative thinking, he built up a list of 300 things to change in his practice. For example:

- He redesigned his office to provide maximum comfort to the "short people" who came there. He lowered the reception staff into a pit behind the counter, so they were at eye level with the patients.
- He hung giant photographs of each dentist and dental assistant along with descriptions of each person's hobbies and interests, so new patients could pick their dentists and D.A.s based on having something in common with them.
- He gave away free bicycles! Every patient got a "home care follow-through Report Card" for his or her parents to fill out. If the Report Card came back to the dentist with all As, the youngster got a bicycle. (Imagine—as little Johnny rides around the neighborhood on his new bike and people ask him who got it for him, he answers, "My dentist.")
- He called each new patient at home the evening after treatment, just to see how the patient was feeling. He called each parent the day after the child's treatment.
- Each new patient left the office the first time with an autographed 8 by 10 inch glossy of his dentist and dental assistant!

Guess what? At backyard barbecues, PTA meetings, office lunches—the number one topic of conversation was little

Johnny's weird dentist! Pardon the pun, but his practice multiplied itself by 10 purely through word-of-mouth advertising.

A stands for *ASK.* I am amazed at the wimpiness of most businesspeople, salespeople, and professionals when it comes to the simple act of asking for referrals. I believe there is a Biblical instruction about this.

Here are the four best ways to ask for referrals:

1. DISPLAY AND CONVEY YOUR EXPECTATIONS.
In doctors' offices, we encourage the use of some kind of "display board" listing the names of the patients who have referred that month. This list says to everyone who sees it: "Our patients refer—we expect you to refer also." It works. And it can be copied by an endless variety of retail businesses.

2. CONDUCT REFERRAL PROMOTIONS.
Give your customers cards, coupons, or certificates good for gifts or discounts that they can endorse, like a check, and give to their friends and colleagues. Then give away prizes to those who generate the most referrals within a certain period.

A clothing store that used this technique got over 100 new customers in 90 days in exchange for the expense of one getaway weekend, six new suits as second prizes, and the cost of printing up the certificates.

3. CONDUCT REFERRAL EVENTS.
An insurance agent I know throws himself a birthday party each year and invites all his clients and all the friends they care to bring to the bash. It's usually held in a huge tent, with live entertainment, a buffet, drinks, wandering magicians, belly dancers, and all sorts of other goings-on. Hundreds of clients bring hundreds

of other people each year—and the birthday boy gets to meet and make friends with hundreds of prospects.

4. SIMPLY ASK.

The most successful insurance professionals I know emulate Paul J. Meyer (founder of Success Motivation Institute* and author of the tape "Prospect Your Way to Millions"), in handing their clients 10 of their business cards and asking for brief notes of introduction to 10 referrals. If you sell face-to-face, person-to-person to your customers or clients, you can and should use this technique.

R stands for *RECOGNIZE* and *REWARD*.

A favorite story: a guy rows his little boat out to the middle of the lake for a relaxing day of fishing. Up over the side of the boat comes a huge green snake, with a half-swallowed frog sticking out of its mouth. Feeling for the frog, the guy whacks the snake with the oar; the snake spits out the frog; the frog's life is saved—and that makes the guy feel good. But the guy also knows he has just deprived the snake of a meal—and that makes him feel bad. Having no food with him, he gives the snake a swig out of his bottle of bourbon, and the snake swims away happy.

Two minutes later the snake swims back with two frogs in its mouth.

When we recognize and reward a certain behavior, we inspire more of the same. It's true in parenting, in managing, and in "managing customers." When you get a referral from a customer or client, the smartest thing you can do is to make a big, big deal out of it. Call with thanks or send a personal thank-you note or gift.

Not long ago, I got a nice referral from a client. I immediately called the Omaha Steaks company and had them Federal Express

---

*The Success Motivation Institute is a publisher and marketer of self-improvement and motivation courses, based in Waco, Texas.

a box of steaks to the guy. He called and told me that I was the first person in 30 years to actually thank him for a referral. He's since sent me a small fortune in referral business.

ULTIMATE MARKETING SECRET WEAPON #17
A "CHAMPION"

Elsewhere in this book I told you about the best car salesman I know, Bill Glazner. He has never yet asked me for a referral, but he is so darned good at what he does that I have sent him several dozen customers. And he has thanked me for every one of them.

In me, he has created a "champion"—a person who champions his cause, who tells everybody about him. A handful of cultivated, appreciated champions can make you rich.

11

CREATING SHORT-TERM SALES SURGES

Each business hits its own times of need when a sales surge is important. It's always preferable to sell your way out of a financial problem than to borrow or to sell off equity. Often that can be done.

Here are the best ways I know to create a short-term sales surge.

BIG DISCOUNT, BELIEVABLE REASON WHY

Excess inventory, out-of-date inventory, service time during the off-season . . . such merchandise can often be sold at big discounts, but it's important to remember the current high level of skepticism and cynicism of your public. Many outstanding discount offers fail miserably because the intended buyers "smell a rat."

When you run a fire sale, they'd better be able to see the charred timbers!

When you offer an exceptional savings opportunity, there'd better be a good reason. Here are a few "good reasons":

- We're offering this value only to our best customers, as a reward for their support.
- We're extending this offer only to new, first-time customers.
- Frankly, this is our slowest month and to avoid laying off our great employees we'd rather offer you an exceptional value. (There's an upholstery shop in my city that runs this promotion every July with great success.)
- We've been given a special incentive from the factory, and we're passing that savings on to you.
- We're eager to show you our new (whatever) and thought that offering this exceptional value would be a good enticement.

SWEEPSTAKES WINNERS

Want to get past, inactive customers back into your place of business? All your customers in this week? I got this in the mail, and the headline immediately grabbed me:

FINALLY—YOU ARE A SWEEPSTAKES WINNER

I don't know about you, but I enter all those darned magazine company sweepstakes. I go for the Readers Digest sweepstakes, and I buy my weekly lottery tickets—after all, as a character in the movie *Let It Ride* said, "You could be walking around lucky and not know it." In a lot of years, though, I have gone winless. Ed McMahon has not called me. But the headline *FINALLY—YOU ARE A SWEEPSTAKES WINNER* got me. I read that letter. And if you send a letter to every one of your customers with that headline on it, every one of them will read it.

Now, what should the letter say? Here's an example, courtesy of Gary Halbert:

Dear Valued Customer:

I am writing to tell you that your name was entered into a drawing here at my store and you have won a valuable prize.

As you know, my store, ABC Jewelry, specializes in low-cost, top-quality diamond rings and diamond earrings. Well, guess what? The other day we got in a small shipment of fake diamonds that are made with a new process that makes them look so real they almost fooled me!

Anyway, I don't want to sell these fakes because they could cause a lot of trouble for the pawnbrokers around town. So I've decided to give them away to some of my good customers whose names were selected at random by having my wife, Janet, put all the names in a jar and pull out the winners.

So, you're one of the winners—and all you've got to do is drop in sometime before 5:00 PM Friday and you'll have a 1-karat "diamond" that looks so good it'll knock your eyes out!

Sincerely,

John Jones

P.S.: After 5:00 PM Friday, I reserve the right to give your prize to someone else. Thank you.

With some variation of this idea, you can get all your customers to flood your store within a short period of time. Then, if you have new products or special offers ready and waiting, the cash register'll ring happily.

THE RED-TAG SALE

"It's inventory clearance time and we're closing all day Friday to go through the stores and place new red tags on as many items as possible, each with the lowest price ever offered on it. Only a certain number of each red-tag item will be available, on a first-come, first-satisfied basis. The red-tag sale starts at 10:00 AM Saturday morning. Red tags will disappear all day long. The later in the day, the fewer the red tags."

That's the basic pitch for a red-tag sale. These tend to work well once or twice a year for retail businesses.

COUPONS, DOUBLE COUPONS, AND CHECKS

Lots of people buy the newspaper on certain days just to get all the grocery store and manufacturers' coupons inside. They carefully go through all this coupon-driven advertising and inserts, scissors in hand, with buying on their minds. You can capitalize on this with an ad or insert on this day that is made up of coupons and looks like all the other coupon advertising.

If I had a shoe store, for example, my Sunday newspaper insert might be a page of coupons: one for boys' shoes, one for girls' shoes, one for men's, etc.

There's usually at least one supermarket in each area that advertises a "Double Coupon Day," when all manufacturers' coupons are accepted and doubled; a 50¢-off coupon becomes worth $1-off.

If you accept manufacturers' coupons, this is a promotion worth considering. If not, there may be another way you can use the same idea. You might, for example, send a letter to your customer list in advance of your coupon-type newspaper ad advising them of its impending appearance and giving them a card or certificate that doubles the value of the coupons.

I saw a fast-food chain put up signs outside all its stores while Burger King, its competitor, was running a big coupon promotion:

WE ACCEPT
BURGER KING COUPONS
AND
GIVE DOUBLE VALUE!

If mailing to customers for a special sale, consider enclosing a "real" check, made out to your own store, with the customer's name on it where the signature belongs. The check is redeemable at your store but otherwise useless. There's something psychologically challenging about throwing out a check.

THE PREMIUM MAKES THE DIFFERENCE

Find a wholesale source for one or more very desirable, appealing premiums and you can build a surge around the "free gift" you offer.

Television sets and jewelry are very effective premiums, particularly around Christmas. Getaway weekend packages work well for car dealers. The most interesting one I've ever seen: a free Mustang convertible with purchase of a Rolls Royce. One outstanding source of low-cost premium merchandise is the closeout merchandise industry. This industry has its own trade shows, newspaper, and catalog companies. If you are not familiar with this, information is available from my office.

THE "MY ACCOUNTANT THINKS I'M CRAZY" SALE

Sometimes humor works in marketing. I've used this myself, in sale promotions for my mail-order company, and I've seen both retailers and service providers use it effectively.

A tongue-in-cheek ad or letter talks about your annoyance at your nagging, domineering, penny-pinching, Scrooge-ish accountant, how he bullies you, pushes you around, and watches you like a hawk . . . but now that he's out-of-town on vacation for the week, you're going to have some fun . . . with the wildest, most generous offers in the history of your business . . .

SPORTS-RELATED PROMOTIONS

America loves its sports activities, and sports are always on the minds of a lot of people, so tie-in promotions get favorable attention. For several years in a row, I've run a "triple play" promotion for my mail order company, offering a "buy one, get two free" deal to my best customers. This is the same as a 67 percent discount, but three for one sounds a lot bigger. And I tie the whole thing to baseball, either early in spring or at World Series time, with free baseball cards, baseball terminology and clip-art, and so on. *IT'S TRIPLE PLAY TIME* has pulled as much as a 70 percent response from my customers!

TRADE-INS

Trade-in promotions are, of course, standard in the automobile business and common with sewing machines, vacuum cleaners and automobile batteries—but there are lots of other businesses that could use this technique, including office equipment; television, stereo, and electronics; clothing, with the trade-ins going to the Salvation Army. A spa selling memberships could accept old exercise equipment.

EASY PAYMENT TERMS

If you cover your costs, why not finance your profits? Let's say you want to feature and sell a $300 item that costs you $100. You might offer your customers this deal: $100 down, then four monthly payments of $50 each, no interest, no carrying charges. Just have them place their VISA card, MasterCard, or American Express Card numbers with you and sign a simple statement authorizing you to charge their credit cards each month automatically.

You can apply the same structure to hitting a certain size of purchase; buy $500 or more and we'll finance two-thirds of the sale.

In Canada, it's common for home mortgages to be set up with payments twice a month instead of once a month, because most wage earners get paid twice a month. If you set up any of your own financing, you might consider doing the same thing. Smaller payments every two weeks may be more appealing than one larger payment once a month.

CELEBRITY APPEARANCES

A surge of customers can be drawn to one retail location within just a few hours by promoting the appearance of a celebrity or celebrities, including local radio or TV personalities, players from the local pro teams, a beauty pageant winner, race car driver, or similar "star."

It has become common practice in the go-go bar business to bring in a *Penthouse* centerfold or an adult-movie starlet for one night (and one night only!) and heavily promote her appearance all month long to regular customers and to the public. Clubs that normally draw a hundred customers in a night can draw a thousand with this technique.

Retail merchants in a shopping center or neighborhood can pool their resources to arrange and promote a celebrity appearance.

NEW MARKETING
TECHNOLOGIES

Some of the newest technologies offer tremendous opportunities for creative marketers. Here are my favorites:

THE NONTHREATENING FIRST CONTACT

A prospective customer or client sees your ad or receives your mailing, is interested but, for one reason or another, still reluctant to call you directly and ask questions. Why not offer this person an option—a nonthreatening first contact. There are voice mail services and systems that will play recorded messages of any length and, if desired, take messages or, at the caller's option indicated by pushing a number, transfer her to your main number.

Using one of these recorded messages, you can advertise that number and give people the option of first hearing additional details. Using recorded messages, you can make this information accessible 24 hours a day, seven days a week. Using recorded messages, you can run smaller ads, thus saving money.

Let's take the auto repair shop owner who wants to advertise in the newspaper, but can't afford to run ads big enough to tell his story. So he runs this relatively small ad:

> BEFORE YOU GO ANYWHERE FOR AUTO REPAIRS:
> FREE RECORDED MESSAGE REVEALS
> FOUR SECRETS TO GETTING YOUR MONEY'S WORTH
> CALL: 000-0000

You'll see more and more of this. In the real estate industry, my clients Craig Proctor and Craig Forte, both advisors to Realtors, have taught thousands of agents how to beef up response to their ads with this strategy. I know of very successful uses in advertising carpet cleaning, pest control, remodeling, and other home services; chiropractic, dental, podiatry, and other health services; cruises, Las Vegas vacations, and other travel services; business opportunities and franchises; retail stores' sales and special events; and the list goes on and on.

SMART WAYS TO USE THE INTERNET

The Internet is a horribly over-hyped area of opportunity. But I can suggest several tested, proven, practical, and almost universally valuable uses:

First, create a Web site for your business not so much as a means of acquiring customers via Cyberspace, but as a customer service, education, and information center. For example, I helped one manufacturer cut down incoming calls with questions about assembly, use, and troubleshooting by nearly 40 percent (saving over $100,000 in staff expense) by putting answers to all the commonly asked questions, diagrams, etc. up on a Web site accessible free, 24 hours a day. You can even make a portion of your site "access restricted," for customers, clients, subscribers, or "members" only, adding mystique to your marketing, and adding perceived value for your clientele: a restaurant could do this with "secret recipes" and special VIP offers; a clothing retailer with etiquette and fashion tips and special offers, and so on. Of course, you'll also want a promotional area on your site designed for new customers, and you'll then want to add your Web site address to your advertising and marketing materials.

Second, begin collecting and organizing the e-mail addresses of your customers and collecting the e-mail addresses of visitors to your site.

With this list, you can do virtually free, push button marketing anytime you like, as often as you like. You can send out an e-mail newsletter to your customers, or other information, like tip sheets.

Let's say you have a rather ordinary business; heating and cooling repair, for example. Here are a few of the things you might transmit by e-mail to your customer list:

1. Prepare for winter/prepare for summer info
2. Insulation and energy efficiency tips
3. Long-term weather forecasts gleaned from Farmers Almanac
4. Special offers for seasonal check-ups, maintenance plans
5. New product information

Third, in seeking publicity from the media, being able to fax, e-mail or mail VERY brief, provocative news releases that refer the recipients to your Web site for more information is very useful.

Everybody in the media *is* on-line. And, bluntly, they're lazy, so if they can research a story without leaving their chair, believe me, that's the way they're going to do it. If you go the route of writing articles for publication in your industry journals, you can even post a whole collection of them on your site, and invite any publication to download and use whatever they like.

Here is a summation of my recent advice to most business owners about the Internet: do NOT be seduced, do NOT buy into the hype and expect miracles or invest inordinate amounts of time or money. Do NOT let the Internet take away from your commitment to more reliable, predictable, results-measurable advertising and marketing media. But DO get involved. At whatever pace is comfortable for you, begin learning about the Internet, getting your business on the Net, and experimenting with practical applications like those I just described. Proceed calmly, deliberately, strategically.

MORE WILL LISTEN THAN WILL READ

As a consultant, I've developed "Audio Brochures"—promotional audiocassettes—for franchisors and business-opportunity marketers, service businesses, ad agencies, investment counselors, newsletter publishers, planned-community developers, politicians, and dozens of other marketers. In the multi-level marketing industry, over 2 million copies of the Audio Brochures I've created have been distributed. A well-done Audio Brochure offers a number of important advantages, notably these:

1. MANY MORE PEOPLE WILL LISTEN THAN WILL READ.
Right now, about one third of all adult Americans are functionally illiterate, and that number includes both blue-collar and white-collar workers; both dropouts and college grads; both men and women. I recently worked on a TV infomercial starring *Lethal Weapon* actor Danny Glover promoting an adult literacy course and have had the opportunity to talk with many illiterate adults as well as some of the experts in this field. I can tell you that this is a problem no marketer can afford to ignore. There's also a convenience factor at work here: we are a very busy society and many people will not invest their time in reading a solicitation. They will, however, listen.

2. HIGH PERCEIVED VALUE.
Recipients value an audiotape—it is not "junk mail" or just another brochure. People are unlikely to discard it without listening.

3. CONTROL OF YOUR PRESENTATION.

It's difficult to skim an audiotape. Most people listen to it from beginning to end. You control the order in which they get your information. You can deliver it with voice inflection, enthusiasm, even music and sound effects.

4. DELIVER A MORE COMPLETE PRESENTATION.

An Audio Brochure can deliver about 250 words a minute; 2,500 words in ten minutes to 7,500 words in 30 minutes. Prospects will listen to ten, 20-, and 30-minute audio messages—it's much tougher to get them to read 2,500 to 7,500 words!

5. REPETITION.

Our own experience and that of our clients indicates that many prospects listen to an Audio Brochure several times and then respond positively. You might say that they are getting themselves sold, at their own pace.

A good Audio Brochure can be professionally recorded and produced for under $1,000 in nonrecurring costs, then duplicated for 60¢ to $1 each.

VIDEO BROCHURES AND INFOMERCIALS

The most powerful medium on earth is television. Want proof? Monica Lewinsky's two-hour TV interview by Barbara Walters not only shot Monica's tell-all book to the top of the bestseller lists, but in a rather odd demonstration of this media's influence, it made the brand and shade of lipstick Monica was wearing the number one selling lipstick in America overnight.

HBO had a comedy series called *Dream On*, in which lead character Martin Tupper thought in soundbites and images from all the TV sitcoms and movies he watched while growing up, plunked in front of the set for hours each day. He responded to just about every event by seeing and hearing a clip from one of the old shows. It was a clever premise and a very funny program, but it is also a powerful reminder of just how much we are influenced by television.

Because we are conditioned to watch "talk shows" for information and entertainment, a whole new advertising mechanism—the 30-minute long infomercial—has turned into a billion-dollar industry relying on the talk show format to sell everything from self-improvement courses to car polish.

I've been involved with the production of nearly a hundred of these infomercials, many featuring Hollywood and sports celebrities, and can attest to their incredible power. Shows I've worked on like Acne-Statin or Pro-Activ, both acne treatments, have literally created huge brands and businesses, with reach far beyond the TV screen.

As of the end of 1998, the Pro-Activ series of shows and related direct-mail activities had sold over $40 million worth of products and, more importantly, created tens of thousands of loyal, repeat customers. I developed one infomercial for a small company that tripled its sales and, in five years, made its owner a multi-millionaire—it was, and I think still is, the longest running business opportunity lead generation infomercial in history.

For national marketers, infomercials are aired on national cable networks like Lifetime and the Discovery Channel, as well as local broadcast stations nationwide, and used to sell products directly or to collect leads for follow-up by mail or phone. The shows I've been associated with so far have sold well over $100 million worth of merchandise and have built immensely valuable customer lists.

There are opportunities for smaller businesses, too. For local or regional marketers, infomercials can be aired on local broadcast stations, local cable operations, and regional superstations like WGN. A local chiropractor has a show he produced for under $10,000 that airs in a local market at $500 to $700 per half hour—with an average pay-off of two to three times his media cost in new patients. I produced an infomercial for an Arizona gubernatorial candidate who aired it repeatedly on local broadcast stations throughout the state to get his message out—as well as to raise funds directly via an 800 number advertised on the show. While I can't claim it got him elected—he lost the primary—it did garner a significantly larger vote than he would otherwise have gotten, and it did raise funds. Given a less controversial, less damaged candidate, it's now my conviction that such a show would have paid for its media time in direct contributions, dollar for dollar, thus giving the candidate free advertising. I believe you'll see infomercials growing in use for political campaigning. My friend and colleague, Lee Milteer, has played the host in a series of infomercials produced and aired by a group of Virginia Beach cosmetic surgeons, and the shows have created so much business they can be aired only in short spurts, then rested. Car dealers, travel companies, charities, and an ever-increasing variety of marketers are finding ways to profit from infomercials.

The infomercial duplicated as a Video Brochure is also proving immensely successful as a recruiting tool for multilevel or network marketing companies, and as a sales tool for car manufacturers, computer companies, health-care practitioners, seminar marketers, and a seemingly endless variety of other businesses.

Another increasingly popular advertising technique is to advertise and offer a free video, collect a refundable deposit on a credit card, and send the video out to do the sales job.

One tip about all this: even if producing an audio or video brochure that will never be broadcast, use TV or radio talk show-like formats, not monologues. In other words, package your sales message into an information and entertainment format people have been conditioned to watch or listen to.

THE MAGIC OF DESKTOP PUBLISHING

As a computer-phobic, computer-illiterate, "all thumbs" kind of guy, I am a clumsy but nevertheless enthusiastic fan of desktop publishing as a force in marketing. Desktop Publishing makes it possible, practical, and affordable for small businesses and entrepreneurs to be very sophisticated and creative.

Twenty-five years ago, I was in the typesetting business. For the most part, if a business owner wanted a brochure or flyer or even a good-looking sales letter done, he had to bring it to me, or it would go through a printer or ad agency to me; we'd pick out typestyles, and about $50,000 worth of equipment and a trained typesetting person were required to get the job ready to print. It could easily cost $500 to $2,000 just to get a relatively simple four-page brochure typeset and "camera ready" to print. Today, just about anybody can do that—or do it for you—on an ordinary PC with very inexpensive, off the shelf software in less than half the time.

My own *No B.S. Marketing Letter*, published monthly for thousands of subscribers worldwide, would have taken several days and at least several hundred dollars to get typeset and ready for printing "in the old days." Today, my wife does it on the Mac right here at home in about an hour. Free.

What this means is that you can afford to create a lot of good printed marketing and communication material for your business, and you should. In fact, one great path to "added value" when competing with big, national companies is by being a provider of a lot of useful information and education to your customers. A "customer newsletter" provides that and adds the "personal touch" feeling.

My speaking colleague Elaine Floyd teaches thousands of small business owners how to quickly, easily, and cheaply produce effective newsletters, and I highly recommend her seminars and her kit, titled "Marketing with Newsletters."*

TELEMARKETING BY ROBOT

Consider this diverse list of businesses:

- Burglar alarms
- Barber shop
- Life insurance
- Jewelry store
- Bank
- Carpet cleaning
- Chimney sweep
- Dental care
- Lingerie home parties
- Health spa

- Contact lenses
- Car wash
- Discount pantyhose
- Stocks and bonds
- Closet organizer systems
- Cable TV
- Chiropractor
- Oil portraits
- Restaurant
- Grocery store

Businesses in every one of these and at least 500 other categories have successfully used "auto-dialers" to do telemarketing. An auto-dialer can be programmed with a list of phone numbers or with a phone prefix, and it will then dial thousands of numbers and deliver the message you've set it up with. The machine takes

---

*Information about Elaine Floyd can be found at *www.dankennedy.com.*

no breaks, sick days, or vacations; never complains; and is impervious to rejection.

Many businesses have used auto-dialers to call homes in a given area to prospect for new business. The savviest marketers, in my opinion, also use them to call existent and past customers with new offers and promotions.

These days, there are also service bureaus that will provide this for you, so you do not have to concern yourself with acquiring lists, or buying and operating equipment. One such company is Arch Communications, but there are many—probably including one in your own city.

In some states and communities, laws restrict the use of these machines as well as the services, and you may want to check your area's laws before using this idea.

BROADCAST FAX

Right now, one of the hottest marketing tools I'm using, as are almost all of my clients and hundreds of my Inner Circle Members is broadcast fax. In most cases, you can acquire whatever kinds of business lists you want and have the actual fax sent for under 15 cents per page. Even the local restaurant can afford to send a weekly fax out to all the businesses in its area, with weekly specials, new menu information, and coupons.

But its best use may very well be for lead generation. I have insurance agents, real estate agents, printers, advertising specialty companies, janitorial services, and many other businesses faxing, offering free information, and getting requests back via fax.

There is the likelihood of annoying a few recipients when you broadcast fax, and it's important to give recipients a way to ask to be removed from your list so they do not receive your faxes in the future. You may still get a few complaint faxes or calls. In most situations, this is a small price to pay, considering the incredible effectiveness and cost-effectiveness of this marketing tool.

One of the biggest companies providing lists and broadcast fax services is CyNet*, but there are many others. There are also fax number lists readily available from brokers or even on CD-ROM and software available to do your own broadcast faxing if you prefer.

FOCUS GROUPS

A focus group is a human technology, the bringing together of people, usually representing targeted demographics, showing them commercials, advertising, offers, and products, and collecting their thoughts, reactions, and opinions.

If you hire a professional market-research firm to conduct focus groups for you, they'll usually have some of their analysts and you out of sight behind a one-way glass so you can watch and observe the entire process.

My own experience with focus groups has been only mildly positive. A great many inconsistencies come out of these groups, with one person contradicting another so that there is no conclusive information. This only reinforces the fact that most people do not know and cannot logically enunciate their reasons for buying or not buying, because every sale is made on emotional and subconscious levels as well as on logical and conscious levels.

Just about every focus group, however, does yield one or two consistent, agreed-on ideas, and these are often useful in modifying some aspect of your marketing.

---

*For information on CyNet, see *www.dankennedy.com*.

A better use of this idea is with groups of your own customers. The famous Stew Leonard's supermarket invites groups of its customers in for coffee, doughnuts, and conversation about their likes and dislikes, and they've discovered some real gems by doing this. Such an approach makes a great deal of sense to me, and I think most businesses could benefit by doing this.

THE VALUE OF SCREWING UP

There is only so much you can learn from *other people's experience.* You can observe and investigate and research and consider expert advice, but there are some things you'll never know about for sure unless *you* try them.

The reader of this book who immediately responds with "not for *my* business" when presented with information about broadcast fax or auto-dialers or infomercials does himself an awesome disservice. An open, curious mind is a valuable asset.

Recently, I watched the president of a 47-year-old, $15-million-a-year company, as a seminar attendee, have his marketing problems and goals brainstormed but respond to every suggestion with some reason why it couldn't work for his business. His company, after 47 years in its industry, should have been a $75-million-a-year industry leader, but it isn't and won't ever be as long as Mr. Not-For-Me is in charge.

Every business should assign some time and money to outright, unashamed experimentation.

13

HIRING AND FIRING
THE EXPERTS

The typical businessperson will face a whole array of experts eager to help her—for a price. These notably include advertising agencies and marketing consultants. I have owned an ad agency, I am a marketing consultant, and I'm going to tell you that you've gotta watch out for us!

My friend and colleague Bill Brooks defines "consultant" as somebody who knows 357 sexual positions but can't get a date for Friday night. It's not an unfair characterization.

YOU ARE THE EXPERT

My very best word of caution is this: remember that you are the number one expert in your business. Nobody has the feel for it that you do. And you must never let a hired gun talk you into doing something that feels totally wrong to you. Trust your instincts.

Also, I suggest using experts to do better what you could do if you had to. I think you need to know enough about advertising, marketing, and promotion to do your own before you turn it over to other experts. This way, you can tell good from bad and right from wrong.

It frightens me when a client delegates 100 percent of his marketing decisions to me or some other outsider. I prefer working as a collaborator by matching my marketing expertise with his unequalled understanding of his own business.

ULTIMATE MARKETING SIN #5
ABDICATING CONTROL

If a consultant gets huffy about explaining his reasoning and rationale for his suggestions and his work—shoot him. You have a right to pass judgment on his reasoning.

HOW TO HIRE AN ADVERTISING OR MARKETING PRO

Before you hire an expert, determine that her expert status comes from experience, not theory. I am constantly amused by the consulting firms and ad agencies that employ people directly from college—I'd never, ever, ever hire such a person. There is a night-and-day difference between solving marketing problems in the classroom and in the real world; there is a red-and-green difference between creating an ad in six weeks in the classroom and figuring out how to fix a headline in six minutes under the deadly deadlines of real life. The big-name firms who hire wet-behind-the-ears MBAs do their clients a grave disservice.

I suggest you hire experts with real-world experience: Somebody with bruises and battle scars, who started out at the broom-in-hand level and clawed his way up. Determine whether or not she knows how to sell.

Quite possibly the world's greatest copywriter and direct-marketing wizard, my friend and colleague Gary Halbert has sold encyclopedias door to door, hocked his own furniture to fund his direct-marketing promotions, and proved that he knows how to separate money from customers over and over again, on the street. There isn't an ounce of theory left in his body. Gary can sell ice to Eskimos, concert tickets to the deaf, yachts to desert dwellers, and birth-control pills to Social Security recipients.

He is a *salesperson.* As a result he views all other forms of marketing, advertising, promotion, and publicity as means of making sales.

If I were hiring an ad agency or marketing consultant, I think the first thing I'd want to know is what experience it or he has selling: face-to-face, nose-to-nose, toes-to-toes, bare-knuckle selling.

Let me tell you a little secret about a lot of ad agencies: they hire outside consultants to help them prepare presentations to new clients because, without help, they can't even sell their own services!

Determine whether or not your expert has successful *direct-*marketing experience. That means that, through print or broadcast, she has managed to get people to go to the phone or mailbox and exchange their hard-earned bucks for her products. Any goof can create good institutional (image) advertising. This is no-brainer stuff. Worse, nobody can measure whether it's good or bad. I'd like to hear Goodyear's story of *exactly* how much revenue is produced as a result of the blimp.

Ad agencies love institutional advertising. They hate direct response.

Most ad agencies like to get paid by fees and a percentage of all the money the client spends buying media. Good direct-marketing pros like to get paid based on the sales or results of the campaigns they create. That tells you a lot.

Determine whether or not they have some experience with a business, product, or service similar to yours. I turn down clients with businesses I have no feel for and experience with, and I call that integrity. In the rare cases where I deal with a business that is totally foreign to me, I freely disclose that to the client and I appropriately discount my compensation. I call that integrity, too.

WARNING SIGNS OF EXPERTS TO AVOID
LIKE THE PLAGUE

Not long ago, I was brought in to try to fix an infomercial that had been badly botched by its producers and had proven to be a gold-plated flop. Sitting in the editing facility, I was grumbling and ranting and raving, wondering out loud how anybody could louse up a production so bad.

The editing engineer said, "Let me answer that. The producer told me he thought this project was a loser and his objective was to use the client's money to his own best advantage, to get a few clips that would make his portfolio look good."

Every time I go into an agency with a wall full of awards, I wonder whether they're working for their clients or the award committees. It is worth mentioning that a lot of the advertising that wins awards performs poorly. Agencies that win awards often lose the clients involved in the award-winning campaigns.

Some of the most productive, profitable advertising and marketing in the history of the planet could never qualify for any of the awards. Much of the best marketing gets its results in an ugly way. There may even be a formulaic relationship of awards to profitable results for clients. If there is, it'd be: the fewer awards, the better the clients' results.

Along these same lines, aversion to long copy and a love of "white space" is a dead-bang giveaway of an inept expert.

A client of mine, I, and a guy trying to sell my client on joining a new advertising co-op were having lunch. The co-op guy spent 10 minutes criticizing my client's current ad, telling him it was too cluttered, had much too much copy, and so on. When he finally shut up, my client innocently responded: "Well, maybe you're right. It only pulls an eight-times return on investment. How much better do you think your group will do?"

The poor guy almost needed the Heimlich maneuver.

Take a look at the work being done by the pro you're thinking about hiring and see how closely it conforms to the principles presented in my book *The Ultimate Sales Letter*. If your pro's copywriting methods differ greatly from those described in my book—run! That may sound arrogant, maybe even closed-minded, but I won't retract it.

Now here's the big danger signal: refusal or reluctance to provide a number of satisfied, successful clients you can call and talk to. Certainly there are instances where confidentiality precludes a consultant from revealing clients. That does exist. But it is the exception, not the norm. Any ad agency or marketing pro worth his salt should be able to provide a number of good references and, when checked out, those references should be thrilled with the work of the consultant. Anything less than this is simply unacceptable. Get and check references.

HOW TO GET MORE INFORMATION FROM THE AUTHOR

For a catalog of Dan Kennedy's books, audiocassette courses, marketing tool kits, and other products, you can visit *www.kimble-kennedypublishing.com* or call toll-free, 1-800-223-7180.

For information about joining Dan Kennedy's Inner Circle and receiving his *No B.S. Marketing Newsletter*, you can visit *www.dankennedy.com*, fax a request to (602) 269-3113 or phone (602) 997-7707.

For more information about any of the other authors, experts, or suppliers mentioned throughout this book, you can visit *www.dankennedy.com* and access *The Ultimate Marketing Plan Book/Resources & Updates Section* free of charge.

This special section of the author's Web site has been set up and is frequently updated, specifically for readers of this book.

For information about having Dan speak to your association or company's convention or meetings, or about Dan's consulting and direct-response copywriting services, please call (602) 997-7707.

A schedule of open-to-the-public seminars where Dan is speaking is also available on request.

To obtain the companion book, *The Ultimate Sales Letter*, visit your favorite bookstore, access an Internet bookstore, or *www.kimble-kennedypublishing.com*.

ULTIMATE MARKETING PLAN THINK-SHEETS

Here is a fill-in-the-blank summary of the steps, principles, and ideas presented in the book, to help you develop your own Ultimate Marketing Plan. You may want to go through this exercise annually, every six months, every three months, or even monthly, depending on the size, nature, and maturity of your business. Following these blank sheets is a set of completed Think-Sheets for an Italian Restaurant.

MESSAGE

1. RESEARCH ON COMPETITION AND SIMILAR BUSINESS, PRODUCTS AND SERVICES:

Their features, benefits, claims, USPs, etc.:

1. _____	9. _____
2. _____	10. _____
3. _____	11. _____
4. _____	12. _____
5. _____	13. _____
6. _____	14. _____
7. _____	15. _____
8. _____	16. _____

2. FEATURES AND BENEFITS OF YOUR BUSINESS, PRODUCT, OR SERVICE:

Feature	Benefit
1. _____	1. _____
2. _____	2. _____
3. _____	3. _____
4. _____	4. _____
5. _____	5. _____
6. _____	6. _____
7. _____	7. _____

8. _____   8. _____

9. _____   9. _____

10. _____   10. _____

11. _____   11. _____

12. _____   12. _____

13. _____   13. _____

14. _____   14. _____

15. _____   15. _____

16. _____   16. _____

17. _____   17. _____

18. _____   18. _____

19. _____   19. _____

20. _____   20. _____

3. UNIQUE SELLING PROPOSITION
Describe:

_____

_____

Write 3 different headlines based on your USP:

1. _____

2. _____

3. _____

4. IRRESISTIBLE OFFER(S)

Develop one or more irresistible offers compatible with your USP and summarize each offer in twenty words or less:

1. _____

2. _____

3. _____

PRESENTATION

1. THE FIVE STEPS

Explain the need of your customer:

_____

_____

Explain the general "thing" that fulfills that need:

_____

_____

Explain why your product, service, or business is the best "thing":

_____

_____

Justify your price:

_____

_____

Give the reasons the customers should act now:

_____

_____

2. HOW CAN YOU BUILD THE CUSTOMER'S INTEREST IN YOUR PRODUCT, SERVICE, OR BUSINESS

At least five ideas:

1. _____

2. _____

3. _____

4. _____

5. _____

3. SET UP YOUR CALL TO ACTION

What do you want the customer to do? (options)

1. _____

2. _____

3. _____

TARGETS

1. DESCRIBE YOUR GEOGRAPHIC TARGET MARKET:

_____

_____

_____

2. DESCRIBE YOUR DEMOGRAPHIC TARGET MARKET:

_____

_____

_____

3. DESCRIBE YOUR ASSOCIATION/AFFINITY TARGET
MARKET(S):

_____

_____

_____

PROOF

1. LIST ALL THE TYPES OF "PICTORIAL PROOF" YOU HAVE:

1. _____

2. _____

3. _____

4. _____

5. _____

2. LIST ALL THE "TESTIMONIAL PROOF" YOU HAVE:

Real People:

1. _____

2. _____

3. _____

Celebrities:

1. _____

2. _____

3. _____

3. LIST THE "REFERENCE PROOF" YOU HAVE:

1. _____

2. _____

3. _____

4. LIST THE "DEMONSTRATION PROOF" YOU HAVE:

1. _____

2. _____

3. _____

5. LIST ANY OTHER PROOF YOU HAVE:

1. _____

2. _____

3. _____

6. DESCRIBE THE GUARANTEE(S) YOU OFFER:

1. _____

2. _____

3. _____

IMAGE

1. NOTES RE: APPEARANCE OF BUSINESS PREMISES

_____

_____

2. NOTES RE: BUSINESS PREMISES FACILITATING BUYING

_____

_____

3. NOTES RE: COMMUNITY AFFAIRS

_____

_____

4. NOTES RE: CELEBRITY SPOKESPERSON(S)

_____

_____

5. NOTES RE: BRAND-NAME IDENTITY

_____

_____

PUBLICITY

1. CHARITY/NONPROFIT CONNECTION IDEAS:

_____

_____

2. PERSONAL SELF-PROMOTION IDEAS:

_____

_____

3. POSITIONING AS AN EXPERT:

_____

_____

4. CREATIVE PROMOTIONS TO MEDIA:

_____

_____

5. TALK SHOWS:

_____

_____

6. PRESS KIT:

_____

_____

MALIBU-ISM: STAYING HOT

1. PLANNED/BUILT-IN CONSTANT CHANGE
What's New?
* 30 days from now:

_____

* 60 days from now:

_____

* 90 days from now:

_____

2. SEASONAL PROMOTIONS
To-do List:

_____

_____

CALENDAR WEEKS:

1. _____
2. _____
3. _____
4. _____
5. _____
6. _____
7. _____
8. _____
9. _____
10. _____
11. _____
12. _____
13. _____
14. _____
15. _____
16. _____
17. _____
18. _____
19. _____

20. _____

21. _____

22. _____

23. _____

24. _____

25. _____

26. _____

27. _____

28. _____

29. _____

30. _____

31. _____

32. _____

33. _____

34. _____

35. _____

36. _____

37. _____

38. _____

39. _____

40. _____

41. _____

42. _____

43. _____

44. _____

45. _____

46. _____

47. _____

48. _____

49. _____

50. _____

51. _____

52. _____

"POOR BOY" MARKETING STRATEGIES

1. INBOUND TELEPHONE PROCEDURES:

_____

_____

2. TELEPHONE UPSELL PROCEDURES:

_____

_____

3. OUTBOUND TELEMARKETING IDEAS:

_____

_____

4. YCDBSOYA—Proactive ideas:

_____

_____

5. CO-OP PROJECTS:

_____

_____

6. WINDOW DISPLAYS:

_____

_____

7. "TEASER" NEWSPAPER ADVERTISING:

_____

_____

MAXIMIZING CUSTOMER VALUE

1. HONORED GUEST GREETING PROCEDURES:

_____

_____

2. PRODUCT KNOWLEDGE—TEAM TRAINING:

_____

_____

3. POLICY CONTROL:

_____

_____

4. COMPLAINT-RESOLUTION PROCESS:

_____

_____

5. CUSTOMER-RETENTION PLAN:

_____

_____

REFERRALS

1. *E*ARN—Ideas:

_____

_____

2. *A*SK—Ideas:

How can we convey our expectations?

_____

_____

Referral Promotions:

_____

_____

Referral Events:

_____

_____

3. *R*ECOGNIZE AND REWARD:

_____

_____

SALES SURGES

1. BIG DISCOUNT, REASON WHY—Ideas:

_____

_____

2. SWEEPSTAKES WINNERS—Ideas:

_____

_____

3. RED-TAG SALE—Ideas:

_____

_____

4. COUPONS—Ideas:

_____

_____

5. PREMIUMS—Ideas:

_____

_____

6. CRAZY ACCOUNTANT SALE—Ideas:

_____

_____

7. SPORTS-RELATED PROMOTIONS—Ideas:

_____

_____

8. TRADE-INS—Ideas:

_____

_____

9. E-Z PAYMENT TERMS—Ideas:

_____

_____

10. CELEBRITY APPEARANCES—Ideas:

_____

_____

NEW TECHNOLOGIES

1. NONTHREATENING FIRST CONTACT/RECORD MESSAGE—
Ideas:

_____

_____

2. INTERNET—Ideas:

_____

_____

3. AUDIO BROCHURE—Ideas:

_____

_____

4. VIDEO BROCHURE—Ideas:

_____

_____

5. INFOMERCIAL—Ideas:

_____

_____

6. DESKTOP PUBLISHING/MARKETING—Ideas:

_____

_____

7. ROBOT TELEMARKETING—Ideas:

_____

_____

8. FOCUS GROUPS—Ideas:

_____

_____

9. EXPERIMENT!—Ideas:

_____

_____

MESSAGE

1. RESEARCH ON COMPETITION AND SIMILAR BUSINESS, PRODUCTS AND SERVICES

Their features, benefits, claims, USPs, etc.:

1.	Intimate, romantic atmosphere	9.	Fresh seafood daily
2.	Award winning chefs	10.	Major credit cards
3.	Banquet Rooms available	11.	Casual atmosphere
4.	Catering available	12.	
5.	Take-out	13.	
6.	Nightly specials	14.	
7.	Homemade Pasta	15.	
8.	Extensive menu	16.	

2. FEATURES AND BENEFITS OF YOUR BUSINESS, PRODUCT, OR SERVICE:

	Feature		Benefit
1.	Award winning chef	1.	Chef's Nightly Specials
2.	Homemade pasta	2.	All pasta made daily (fresh)
3.	Fresh seafood flown in daily	3.	Fresh seafood choice every day
4.	Extensive menu	4.	Extensive menu guarantees
5.		5.	"Something for Everybody"
6.	Take-Out	6.	Call ahead and take-out
7.	Take-Out	7.	Orders accepted by FAX

8. Major credit cards accepted _____

9. Banquet Facilities _____

10. _____

11. _____

12. _____

13. _____

14. _____

15. _____

16. _____

17. _____

18. _____

19. _____

20. _____

8. All major credit cards welcome _____

9. Complete Banquets for 10 to 1,000 people _____

10. _____

11. _____

12. _____

13. _____

14. _____

15. _____

16. _____

17. _____

18. _____

19. _____

20. _____

3. UNIQUE SELLING PROPOSITION
Describe:

We offer both a "Gourmet Room" with a formal, candlelight atmosphere and strolling

violinists and a "Casual Dining" Enclosed Patio.

_____

Write 3 different headlines based on your USP:

1. Gourmet Italian Dining—Elegant or casual atmosphere.

2. Two great Italian restaurants in one.

3. _____

4. IRRESISTIBLE OFFER(S)

Develop one or more irresistible offers compatible with your USP and summarize each offer in twenty words or less:

1. Lobster and pasta for 2, just $8.95 each, on the patio or in the dining room.

2. Free bottle of house wine for each table, Wednesday nights.

3. _____

PRESENTATION

1. THE FIVE STEPS

Explain the need of your customer:

(1) Dinner   (2) Dining out

(3) Entertainment   (4) Good Food

Explain the general "thing" that fulfills that need:

An evening at a fine restaurant

Explain why your product, service, or business is the best "thing":

An evening at "Gusippe's" provides fine food, choice of atmosphere

Justify your price:

Less than people expect—many $15.95 complete dinners

Give the reasons the customers should act now:

2-for-1 Special

2. HOW CAN YOU BUILD THE CUSTOMER'S INTEREST IN YOUR PRODUCT, SERVICE, OR BUSINESS
At least five ideas:

1. Story about our chef

2. Awards won by restaurant and/or chef

3. Show: Choice of 2 atmospheres

4. _____

5. _____

3. SET UP YOUR CALL TO ACTION
What do you want the customer to do? (options)

1. Call for reservations

2. Come in

3. Call for menu and brochure

TARGETS

1. DESCRIBE YOUR GEOGRAPHIC TARGET MARKET:

West side suburbs

_____

_____

2. DESCRIBE YOUR DEMOGRAPHIC TARGET MARKET:

White collar upper-middle income

_____

_____

3. DESCRIBE YOUR ASSOCIATION/AFFINITY TARGET MARKET(S):

Chamber of Commerce

Italian-American club

5th Street Merchants Assoc

PROOF

1. LIST ALL THE TYPES OF "PICTORIAL PROOF" YOU HAVE:

1. Photographs of "2 Atmospheres"
2. Photographs of meals
3. Photographs of pasta being made on premises
4. _____
5. _____

2. LIST ALL THE "TESTIMONIAL PROOF" YOU HAVE:

Real People:

1. _____
2. _____
3. _____

Celebrities:

1. The Mayor eats here often
2. Channel 3's TV Weatherman
3. _____

3. LIST THE "REFERENCE PROOF" YOU HAVE:

1. List of banquet Clients

2. _____

3. _____

4. LIST THE "DEMONSTRATION PROOF" YOU HAVE:

1. Taste-test our pasta against "Commercial" pasta

2. _____

3. _____

5. LIST ANY OTHER PROOF YOU HAVE:

1. 12 years in business at same location

2. Awards

3. _____

6. DESCRIBE THE GUARANTEE(S) YOU OFFER:

1. Complete satisfaction or dinner's on us.

2. Guaranteed seating within 15 minutes of your reservation

3. _____

IMAGE

1. NOTES RE: APPEARANCE OF BUSINESS PREMISES

2 Atmospheres—Unique

Enclosed patio has fountain, flower garden

2. NOTES RE: BUSINESS PREMISES FACILITATING BUYING

Live lobsters in tank

Giant photos of daily specials

3. NOTES RE: COMMUNITY AFFAIRS

4. NOTES RE: CELEBRITY SPOKESPERSON(S)

5. NOTES RE: BRAND-NAME IDENTITY

"Gusippe's Sauce"—in bottles sold at cash register

PUBLICITY

1. CHARITY/NONPROFIT CONNECTION IDEAS:

Provide dinner gift certificates for charity auctions

2. PERSONAL SELF-PROMOTION IDEAS:

3. POSITIONING AS AN EXPERT:

Idea—run a weekly newspaper column of chef's recipes

4. CREATIVE PROMOTIONS TO MEDIA:

Deliver free pasta to all radio hosts during Italian Liberation week

5. TALK SHOWS:

Write a book—"The Sauce Book"

6. PRESS KIT:

MALIBU-ISM: STAYING HOT

1. PLANNED/BUILT-IN CONSTANT CHANGE

What's New?

* 30 days from now:

* 60 days from now:

* 90 days from now:

Special Summer "Lite Dining Menu"

2. SEASONAL PROMOTIONS
To-do List:

_____

_____

CALENDAR WEEKS:

1. New Year's Eve Party

2. _____

3. _____

4. "Australia Week" Shrimp specials

5. Start pushing Valentine's Day

6. Valentine's Day

7. _____

8. Start pushing St. Patrick's Day

9. Green Pasta—St. Patrick's Day

10. Promote Easter Dinner Specials

11. Promote Easter Dinner Specials

12. Easter Dinners

13. Italian Liberation Week

14. Mother's Day

15. _____

16. _____

17. _____

18. _____

19. Father's Day

20. _____

21. _____

22. _____

23. _____

24. _____

25. _____

26. _____

27. _____

28. _____

29. _____

30. _____

31. _____

32. _____

33. _____

34. _____

35. _____

36. _____

37. _____

38. _____

39. _____

40. Columbus Day _____

41. _____

42. Halloween _____

43. _____

44. Thanksgiving _____

45. _____

46. _____

47. Thanksgiving _____

48. Holiday Parties _____

49. _____

50. _____

51. _____

52. Holiday Parties _____

"POOR BOY" MARKETING STRATEGIES

1. INBOUND TELEPHONE PROCEDURES:

Tell about daily Specials   Get name, phone, and address

Choice of Atmosphere

2. TELEPHONE UPSELL PROCEDURES:

3. OUTBOUND TELEMARKETING IDEAS:

Call past customers

4. YCDBSOYA—Proactive ideas:

Active in Chamber, Clubs

Personally go meet each area business owner

5. CO-OP PROJECTS:

_____

_____

6. WINDOW DISPLAYS:

Tie to seasonal themes   Pasta-making machine
_____

Lobsters in tank
_____

7. "TEASER" NEWSPAPER ADVERTISING:

Campaign for "Italian Liberation Week"
_____

_____

MAXIMIZING CUSTOMER VALUE

1. HONORED GUEST GREETING PROCEDURES:

Good Maitre d'
_____

_____

2. PRODUCT KNOWLEDGE—TEAM TRAINING:

Job rotation
_____

Waiters' briefing by chef 1/2 hr. before opening each evening
_____

3. POLICY CONTROL:

Special orders accommodated if at all possible
_____

_____

4. COMPLAINT-RESOLUTION PROCESS:

Turn over to Manager

"No Charge" meal for any unhappy customer

5. CUSTOMER-RETENTION PLAN:

Track customer frequency and recency

Call "Lost" customers

REFERRALS

1. *E*ARN—Ideas:

Outstanding waiters (memory courses)

Daily "White Glove" inspections

2. *ASK*—Ideas:

How can we convey our expectations?

How can we convey our expectations?

Monthly events calendar and newsletter with "Thank You" list of those who referred

Referral Promotions:

"2-for-1 Dinner With a Friend" Cards

Referral Events:

Annual big party, free appetizers, entertainment

3. *R*ECOGNIZE AND REWARD:

"Thank-you" notes

Free appetizer certificate

SALES SURGES

1. BIG DISCOUNT, REASON WHY—Ideas:

Special prices for weeknights

2. SWEEPSTAKES WINNERS—Ideas:

Trip to Italy

3. RED-TAG SALE—Ideas:

4. COUPONS—Ideas:

5. PREMIUMS—Ideas:

_____

_____

6. CRAZY ACCOUNTANT SALE—Ideas:

_____

_____

7. SPORTS-RELATED PROMOTIONS—Ideas:

Monday Night Football, pizza buffet in lounge
_____

_____

8. TRADE-INS—Ideas:

_____

_____

9. E-Z PAYMENT TERMS—Ideas:

Banquets or catered affairs charged to credit card in 3 monthly installments
_____

_____

10. CELEBRITY APPEARANCES—Ideas:

_____

_____

NEW TECHNOLOGIES

1. NONTHREATENING FIRST CONTACT/RECORD MESSAGE—Ideas:

Hear menu—daily specials on special phone numbers

2. INTERNET—Ideas:

3. AUDIO BROCHURE—Ideas:

4. VIDEO BROCHURE—Ideas:

To area companies to show banquet facilities

5. INFOMERCIAL—Ideas:

6. DESKTOP PUBLISHING/MARKETING—Ideas:

Monthly events calendar

7. ROBOT TELEMARKETING—Ideas:

Call all homes in nearby suburb with a special offer

_____

_____

8. FOCUS GROUPS—Ideas:

Survey customers re: new food item ideas

_____

_____

9. EXPERIMENT!—Ideas:

_____

_____

ULTIMATE MARKETING SECRET WEAPONS AND SINS

WEAPONS

1. The great USP (Unique Selling Proposition).
2. Being clearly understood.
3. Carefully and thoroughly eliminate all assumptions.
4. The guts to ask for action every time, in every presentation.
5. Tailoring and delivering your message to the right market.
6. Marketing messages developed with the understanding that recipients will be stubbornly reluctant to believe them.
7. Pictures that prove your case.
8. Image congruency.
9. Constant change.
10. Capture callers' identity and market to them.
11. The telephone upsell.
12. Telemarketing after direct-mail.
13. Asset-sharing for marketing success.
14. Make the customer feel important, appreciated, and respected.

15. Developing new products and services for existent customers instead of getting new customers for existent products and services.
16. Excellence.
17. A "champion."

SINS

1. Being boring.
2. Wasting your weaponry aiming at the wrong targets.
3. Taking your customer's loyalty for granted.
4. Letting a customer leave angry without first exhausting every means at your disposal to resolve the dispute.
5. Abdicating control.

$450 VALUE
FREE BONUSES

On the following pages, you will find two valuable coupons redeemable for specified consulting services directly with the author.

The first is a CRITIQUE CERTIFICATE that entitles you to submit printed marketing material or advertising for your product for Dan's personal review and recommendations.

The second is a MARKETING CHALLENGE CERTIFICATE that entitles you to submit a specific marketing-related question or problem for Dan's feedback.

Certain restrictions apply, as stated on each of the coupons.

FREE
"Marketing Challenge"
Consultation

*Dan S. Kennedy's regular consulting fees are $800.00 per hour. With this form, you are entitled to briefly and concisely describe your biggest Marketing Challenge and Mr. Kennedy will personally respond with suggestions.

My #1 marketing challenge is _____

_____

_____

_____

_____

_____

_____

_____

_____

Name_____

Address _____

City, State, Zip _____

Phone _____ Fax _____

Return To:
Dan S. Kennedy
Kennedy Inner Circle, Inc.
5818 N. 7th St., #103, Phoenix, AZ 85014
Fax: (602) 269-3113

TERMS & CONDITIONS: Certificate expires 12 months from date of purchase. Allow 2 to 4 weeks for Mr. Kennedy's response. Do NOT telephone; consultation given by mail only. Please be advised that any materials submitted for review may be published in any of Mr. Kennedy's authored/edited publications as examples. Submitted materials will not be returned. Do not submit materials or information you are concerned about keeping confidential.

Code: UMP

$100.00 $100.00
CRITIQUE CERTIFICATE

Entitles bearer to submit any single printed piece, brochure, catalog, direct-mail piece, advertisement, or similar promotional material for mail for critique by Dan S. Kennedy.

Name_____

Address _____

City, State, Zip _____

Phone _____ Fax _____

E-mail address _____

Send Certificate and Materials To:
Dan S. Kennedy
Kennedy Inner Circle, Inc.
5818 N. 7th St., #103, Phoenix, AZ 85014
Fax: (602) 269-3113

Terms & Conditions: Certificate expires 12 months from date of purchase. Allow 2 to 4 weeks for Mr. Kennedy's response. Do NOT telephone; consultation given by mail only. Actual finished materials or "rough sketch" and copy for planned material may be submitted. Coupon redeemable only for listed services. Additional consulting may be contracted for, Mr. Kennedy's schedule permitting; fees quoted on request.

Please be advised that any materials submitted for review by Dan Kennedy, including those submitted with critique coupon, may be published in any of Dan Kennedy authored/edited publications, as examples. Also, submitted materials will not be returned. Do not submit materials you are concerned about keeping confidential. © 1999 D.S. Kennedy

Code: UMP

INDEX

FIND MORE ON THIS TOPIC BY VISITING
BusinessTown.com
The Web's big site for growing businesses!

☑ **Separate channels on all aspects of starting and running a business**

☑ **Lots of info on how to do business online**

☑ **1,000+ pages of savvy business advice**

☑ **Complete web guide to thousands of useful business sites**

☑ **Free e-mail newsletter**

☑ **Question and answer forums, and more!**

businesstown.com